Federal and State Court Systems

Federal and State Court Systems

Analysis of History Making Legal Precedent

First Edition

Alice Elizabeth Perry, J.D., Ph.D.
Westfield State University

cognella®
SAN DIEGO

Bassim Hamadeh, CEO and Publisher
John Remington, Executive Editor
Gem Rabanera, Senior Project Editor
Christian Berk, Production Editor
Emely Villavicencio, Senior Graphic Designer
Trey Soto, Licensing Coordinator
Natalie Piccotti, Director of Marketing
Kassie Graves, Vice President of Editorial
Jamie Giganti, Director of Academic Publishing

3970 Sorrento Valley Blvd., Ste. 500, San Diego, CA 9212

Contents

Section III Exemplary Leadership and Challenges for Under-Represented Minorities in the Legal Field   **119**

Preface

I KNOW OF NO TIME IN HUMAN HISTORY where ignorance was better than knowledge." This quote is by famed astrophysicist and author Neil deGrasse Tyson and is as true today as when he uttered it. The knowledge of our history and the story of how our republic came to be needs to be appreciated and understood by students entering the criminal justice and legal fields.

This anthology is written for undergraduate students who are interested in pursuing a career in the law or in the field of criminal justice. It consists of a series of articles from noted experts in the field, and it is divided into three sections. The idea for this anthology came after teaching numerous courses at the undergraduate level on topics that were germane to criminal law and criminal justice. In this age of the ubiquitous cell phone, instantaneous thirty-second news blips, and ephemeral attention spans, professors practically have to perform gymnastic feats to keep their students' attention. This reader is designed to underscore, for undergraduate students, the profundity of our country's beginning and the importance of our system of government as delineated in the U.S. Constitution and the marvel that is our Bill of Rights.

As a former prosecutor handling major felony cases, I know the importance of the Fourth, Fifth, and Sixth Amendments in the criminal justice field; however, merely memorizing the content of these vital amendments always seemed insufficient, as did reading major U.S. Supreme Court cases on these amendments. In order to appreciate their significance, it occurred to me that we needed to start from the beginning—yes, that beginning—by examining not only the history of the amendments found in our Bill of Rights, but the formation of the U.S. Constitution itself. The law is the foundation for all that criminal justice professionals do in the field; the law proscribes and circumscribes what can be done and what cannot be done in criminal investigations. This examination is encompassed in the first section of this reader.

As I found myself working through Cognella Academic Publishing's repository of exemplary articles written by authors in this field, this anthology began to take shape. We start with a longitudinal view of the U.S. Constitution and the Bill of Rights, jump to legal issues relevant to criminal lawyers and law enforcement, and end with a sampling of articles on issues relevant to the field. This last section acknowledges the diversity in the field and includes interviews with diverse leaders in the criminal justice domain. It is my hope that the anthology, composed of various perspectives, will encourage students to critically think about issues. We are, after all, educating future leaders and policy makers in the legal and criminal justice world.

Section I

The Founding of the United States System of Government

Editor's Introduction

The first section of *Federal and State Court Systems* consists of articles examining the series of compromises involved in setting up our system of government. The first article, "Federalism at the Founding," is an analysis of how our federal system and state system evolved. The issue of federal and state sovereignty reveals the struggles between the large land mass states versus the smaller states. The disputes and contentions of the state representatives is revealed as is the dichotomy between those proposing a strong national government and those advocating for strong states' rights.

The second article examines judicial politics, important concepts like *stare decisis* and the judicial role, and common law. The author does an excellent job of outlining the sources of law in the United States. The analysis is thorough and superbly written.

The last article in this section delves into the history of how our Bill of Rights came to be. It is a fascinating read and should be required reading for those contemplating a career in criminal justice. Criminal justice professionals will work with the Fourth Amendment, the Fifth Amendment, and the Sixth Amendment throughout their careers. The application of these fundamental rights should be deeply appreciated by future practitioners, so they do not give them short shrift. Our nation rests on these bedrock principles.

Federalism at the Founding

David B. Robertson

N O ONE AT THE CONSTITUTIONAL CONVENTION of 1787 fully anticipated or welcomed the federal framework they placed in the U.S. Constitution. The specific rules of American federalism in that document resulted from the delegates' conflicts over the direction of American political development. Most of the Constitution's framers were skilled republican politicians who agreed that the national government needed more power, but they strongly disagreed about how much power the national government needed, and how much power the states should keep. Supporters of broad nationalism, like James Madison of Virginia, aimed to create a very powerful national government, exercising complete power to tax, govern commerce, and defend the nation. These delegates sought to reduce the states to a small, secondary role in American government. Supporters of narrow nationalism, like Roger Sherman of Connecticut, insisted that the new national government needed only a few additional, limited powers. They believed that the states should continue to govern most of American life, and that the national government should supplement, not supplant, most of the existing powers of the states.

These clashing visions produced a federal framework built by a series of political compromises that included elements of both broad and narrow nationalism. Advocates of narrow nationalism won many limitations on national power and protections for the states, while supporters of broad nationalism won many new national powers and elastic authority that could be expanded to meet future national needs. The Constitution gave the national government the tools to manage national sovereignty, but made it difficult for the national government to use these powers. It gave the states the power to manage everyday American life, but it amputated some of the states' tools for dealing with public problems. The Constitution left the dividing line between national and state power ambiguous, inviting endless political conflict over the rules of federalism in the United States.

The Self-Governing States in 1787

By 1787 the states were strong, vigorous, independent-minded political societies. Most were more than a century old. Physically isolated from the British monarch and distant from one another, the colonies gradually established their own taxes, judicial systems, and laws governing commerce, crime, and morals. Long accustomed to such self-rule, the colonies readily declared their independence and transformed themselves into separate, self-governing republics even while they battled the British. Eleven states adopted a new, written constitution laying out the basic rules for exercising state government authority (Rhode Island and Connecticut continued to govern under their written colonial charters of the 1660s, which had established a strong measure of self-government). Each state mounted its own military defense, maintained internal order, and established its own tariff, currency, land, trade, and debt policy. Each created relatively democratic governments in which a large share of white males could elect the state legislators who made state laws.[1]

But because each state's history, economy, and culture differed from the rest, each state had different—sometimes opposing—political interests. The Southern states (Georgia, South and North Carolina, and Virginia) nurtured a plantation economy. These states had extensive, fertile lands and a long growing season, and so grew vast quantities of crops like tobacco, rice, and indigo to ship in bulk abroad. These crops, in turn, encouraged large plantations, and the plantations became dependent on slaves. In the middle states (Maryland, Pennsylvania, Delaware, New Jersey, and New York), smaller farms raised more diverse crops, and manufacturing began to develop. New England had relatively poor soil and a harsh climate that made farming more difficult and less profitable. Compared to the South, New England governments fostered fishing, shipbuilding, and commerce to supplement agriculture.[2] By the 1780s, American leaders recognized that New England and the South already had fundamentally different, and conflicting, interests driven by climate, slavery, commerce, and culture.[3] But many other conflicts among the states cut across these issues. Delaware, Rhode Island, Connecticut, and New Jersey resented the abundant lands that the geographically large states, such as Virginia and Pennsylvania, had at their disposal. The slave *trade* divided the South: Georgia and South Carolina demanded more slaves and the continuation of the slave trade, but Virginia and North Carolina already had an adequate population of slaves and were much more supportive of banning the slave imports. States with large ports, such as Philadelphia, New York, and Boston, angered their neighbors in Connecticut, New Jersey, Delaware, and Maryland, whose farmers had to ship and receive goods through these ports and pay other states' taxes.[4]

In the mid-1780s, the states' diversity and self-serving policies seemed to be breaking the newly independent nation apart. States seemed to benefit themselves at the expense of other states and the nation. An acute economic slump in the 1780s made the problem worse.

In response to angry voters, several states relaxed debtors' obligations to lenders and liberally printed paper money. Rhode Island legally limited interest rates, printed an enormous amount of paper currency, and punished creditors who refused to accept this paper money for debts. Creditors in Rhode Island and in other states were outraged. Massachusetts pursued a much more cautious policy, keeping taxes high and enforcing debt obligations. Local sheriffs foreclosed on financially strapped small farmers who could not meet their obligations. Here, anger spilled over into outright rebellion when Revolutionary war veteran Daniel Shays led a small army of outraged western Massachusetts debtors in seizing towns and burning courthouses. Shays's Rebellion seemed to foreshadow a firestorm of anarchy across the nation.[5] Some leaders and newspapers anticipated the crackup of the nation and its reorganization into smaller confederacies.[6] Like other prominent leaders, George Washington blamed the state governments. Their pursuit of narrow self-interest was making "the situation of this great Country weak, inefficient and disgraceful."[7]

Instead of grappling with these problems, the national government seemed paralyzed by them. The Articles of Confederation of 1781 had established national governing authority in a Confederation Congress. The Articles, however, severely restricted Congress's powers. Each state cast a single, equal vote in the Congress, and the rules allowed a few states or even a single state to block Congress from taking action. Only an extraordinary majority of nine states could enact any major defense or financial policies, and only a unanimous vote of the states could change the Articles. The Confederation government had no executive and no court system. Unlike the states, Congress could not impose taxes (though it could borrow money). Its funding depended on "requisitions," that is, requests to the state governments that the states provide Congress with a particular amount of funding. Congress had no power to compel the states to pay these requisitions, however, and by 1786, Congress was broke because states did not pay their share. Though a large majority of states supported efforts to authorize the Confederation Congress to generate revenue by taxing imports, individual states objected to these plans and killed these proposals by denying them a unanimous vote. Powerful European nations posed a potential threat to the United States by land and sea, but Congress could not defend the nation effectively because it could not pay for an army and navy.

Broad and Narrow Nationalism at the Constitutional Convention

By 1786, many American leaders believed that it was urgent to strengthen the national government. Public support was growing for Constitutional changes that could strengthen property rights, increase national security, and stabilize the economy.[8] An inconclusive meeting in Annapolis, Maryland in 1786 called for a Convention of states in Philadelphia in the next year to "render the constitution of the Federal Government adequate to the exigencies of the Union."[9] All the states except Rhode Island sent delegations to the Constitutional Convention, which met from late May to mid-September, 1787.

Fifty-five prominent political leaders, chosen by their state governments, participated in the Constitutional Convention. State governments chose these delegates to be trustworthy stewards of their own interests as well as those of the nation. Nearly all the delegates had served in state legislatures, and some had served as state governor, attorney general, Supreme Court justice, or other prominent state office. Over half had represented their states in the Confederation Congress. The most active leaders of the Convention occupied most of their time with politics and government. Many, such as thirty-six-year-old James Madison and thirty-year-old Alexander Hamilton, were rising young political leaders, ambitious to build and lead a more potent national government.[10] Most went on to prominent careers in the national government they created.[11]

Broad Nationalism

Some of the delegates insisted that the national government be given broad and strong authority to exercise all the important powers of government, and that the states should be reduced to a minor role in American governance. James Madison of Virginia was the chief spokesman for this broad nationalism. Madison had been battling to increase national government power since his arrival in the Confederation Congress in 1780.[12] A skilled and experienced political leader as well as a natural political strategist, Madison believed that the states' autonomy, power, and selfish parochialism were the fundamental flaw in American government. The states were subverting the national interest, crowding out national power, and threatening basic rights.[13] For Madison, the state legislatures' schemes were the "great evils" about which Americans complained the most, and a new national government with broad national powers was the cure.[14] Madison tried to frame the Convention's fundamental choice in stark terms between two alternatives: "a perfect separation & a perfect incorporation, of the 13 States." If the states went their separate ways, "they would be independent nations subject to no law, but the law of nations" and would have "everything to fear from the larger states." But if the Convention recommended a single strong government, the states "would be mere counties of one entire republic, subject to one common law" and the small states "would have nothing to fear" from the larger ones.[15] He believed that the national government should control all commercial and military power, and should have the power to impose any taxes as needed.[16]

Madison was largely responsible for the Virginia Plan, a set of proposals for a complete restructuring of American government that was introduced at the very start of the Convention. The Virginia Plan proposed a revamped government and a vast expansion of national government power. A new national legislature, composed of two houses (eventually named the "House of Representatives" and the "Senate") would have the authority "to legislate in all cases to which the separate States are incompetent, or in which the harmony of the United States may be interrupted by the exercise of individual Legislation." It also would have the remarkable power to veto "all laws passed by the several States, contravening in the opinion of the National Legislature the articles of Union." Madison believed that this national veto was "absolutely necessary to a perfect system" to "control the centrifugal tendency of the States; which, without it, will continually fly out of their proper orbits and destroy the order & harmony of the political system."[17] Unlike the Confederation Congress, the seats in the new House and Senate would be distributed on the basis of population, so the larger the state, the more votes it could cast in each chamber. The voters, not state governments, would directly select members of the new House of Representatives, and the House then would choose U.S. Senators (from a slate of nominees put forward by state governments). Congress would choose the national executive and national judges, thus almost completely eliminating any state role in selecting national leaders.[18]

Madison's allies endorsed this broad nationalism and sharply criticized the states. Gouverneur Morris of Pennsylvania viewed "State attachments, and State importance" as "the bane of this Country. We cannot annihilate; but we may perhaps take out the teeth of the serpents."[19] For Alexander Hamilton of New York, the United States could not create a true national government unless the states surrendered all their authority to the nation. "The general power, whatever be its form, if it preserves itself, must swallow up the State powers," said Hamilton. "Otherwise it will be swallowed up by them."[20] Charles Pinckney of South Carolina proposed to expand the national veto of state laws by authorizing the national government to veto "all laws" that the new Congress "should judge to be improper"; he emphasized that the states "must be kept in due subordination to the nation."[21]

Narrow Nationalism

But other delegates were just as determined to protect most of the existing state government powers and to grant only narrow, limited authority to the national government. These delegates aimed to shield most of the states' self-government that already had existed for decades, and that the states had strengthened since 1776. The advocates of narrow nationalism wanted a stronger national government, but they wanted specific, narrow new powers rather than the broad authority Madison sought. The national government, for example, should have the power to defend the nation when necessary, but the states should control the militias they already had constructed. The national government should administer commerce between the United States and other nations, and among the states, but the states should control commerce and taxes within their borders.

The most passionate opponents of broad nationalism represented the small, economically vulnerable states wedged in between populous Virginia, Pennsylvania, and Massachusetts. Leaders from New Jersey, Connecticut, Delaware, and Maryland, particularly Roger Sherman and Oliver Ellsworth of Connecticut, mounted the most tenacious opposition to Virginia's proposals. These delegates had legitimate worries. Their states lacked ample lands for expansion, good ports for trade, and a large population to ensure their future prosperity. A strong national government controlled by the large and Southern states could harm the rest. States with large ports like Boston, New York, and Philadelphia could legislate a monopoly for themselves, damaging their neighbors.[22] Any national commercial agreement with another nation could give special treatment to the products and industry of a particular state, and impair the market for the products of other states. Delaware's Gunning Bedford accused the Pennsylvania and Virginia delegates of wishing for a government in which their states "would have an enormous & monstrous influence." Bedford asked, "Will not these large States crush the small ones whenever they stand in the way of their ambitions or interested views?"[23]

These opponents of broad nationalism immediately questioned the Virginia Plan, and emphasized the importance of accepting the existing states as established polities that could not be cut out of the nation's fabric. The states "do exist as political Societies," said Connecticut's William Samuel Johnson, and "a Government is to be formed for them in their political capacity, as well as for the individuals composing them."[24] The states were entrenched in American life, with deep roots that could not be destroyed arbitrarily. These advocates of narrow nationalism soon argued that it was not only necessary to take the existing state governments into account, but also that the states were a great national virtue. The states, in their view, had thriving republican governments that American citizens enthusiastically embraced. Ellsworth insisted that the survival of republican government depended on maintaining the vital role of the states, and he doubted that republican government could exist on a national scale, or maintain the happiness of the citizens.[25] He also doubted whether the national government could deal adequately with the local tasks on which domestic happiness depended. Ellsworth said that from the states "alone he could derive the greatest happiness he expects in this life. His happiness depends on their existence, as much as a newborn infant on its mother for nourishment."[26]

The delegates devised a new form of federalism for the United States, using all their political ingenuity to agree on a series of specific compromises between broad and narrow nationalism. This struggle was fought out piecemeal, and no delegates expected the specific results. Two issues especially divided the Convention: the states' representation in Congress, and the extent of power required by the national government.

Inventing Shared State and National Sovereignty

At first, the advocates of broad nationalism seemed to have the upper hand because it was widely assumed that, by definition, sovereignty—public authority in a geographical area—was supreme and could not be shared among different governments. Conventional wisdom held that a new national government, then, would have full sovereignty in the nation, and this sovereign power could not be shared with the states.[27] Hamilton, for example, insisted that "Two sovereignties cannot co-exist within the same limits."[28] "There can be no line of separation dividing the powers of legislation between the State & General Governments," said John Dickinson of Delaware; it was "inevitable that there must be a supreme & august national Legislature."[29] Elbridge Gerry of Massachusetts "urged that we never were independent States … The States & the advocates for them were intoxicated with the idea of their *sovereignty*."[30]

Proponents of narrow nationalism directly challenged this conventional wisdom, and advanced the innovative idea that the state and national governments should and could *share* sovereignty. Roger Sherman argued that the national government need only be given "power to legislate and execute within a defined province." National government authority should be limited to "defense against foreign danger" and internal upheavals, "treaties with foreign nations," and "regulating foreign commerce, & drawing revenue from it."[31] Two weeks into the Convention, representatives from Connecticut, New Jersey, Delaware, Maryland, and New York constructed an alternative to the Virginia Plan that proposed a power-sharing arrangement for the national and state governments. This "New Jersey" Plan (named for the home state of the delegate who initially presented it to the Convention) proposed to maintain the Confederation Congress, to add a national executive and a supreme court, and to authorize a limited set of new national powers very similar to those Sherman advocated. New Jersey's William Paterson defended the plan, linking state sovereignty to equal state representation in Congress. The success of the new government, said Patterson, depended on "the quantum of power collected, not on its being drawn from the States, or from the individuals," so that it did not matter which level of government exercised power.[32] These arguments moved some advocates of the Virginia Plan, such as Virginia's George Mason, to concede that the state governments required some Constitutional defense.[33]

When the Convention rejected the New Jersey plan, its supporters dug in and focused on protecting equal state representation in Congress. All the delegates believed that, if the state governments chose the U.S. Representatives and Senators, these legislators would serve as agents of state interests. Narrow nationalists viewed equal state representation as an essential safeguard for the less populous states, but broad nationalists saw it as a prescription for ensuring the parochialism that had brought the Confederation to its knees. This debate on representation, meanwhile, gradually was forcing the delegates to clarify the novel concept of shared state and national sovereignty. If the states were to "retain some portion of sovereignty," they needed representation in Congress to preserve it.[34] By late June, even Madison's close ally James Wilson agreed that "There is a line of separation" between state and national powers.[35]

Once the delegates had accepted proportional representation in the House of Representatives, Oliver Ellsworth pressed harder for equal state representation in the Senate, summarizing the idea of shared national and state sovereignty with the phrase, "We were partly national; partly federal." For Ellsworth, "proportional representation in the first branch was conformable to the national principle & would secure the large States against the small," while "An equality of voices was conformable to the federal principle and was necessary to secure the Small States against the large."[36] Delegates like Benjamin Franklin were beginning to accept this logic.[37] On July 2, the Convention deadlocked on the issue and delegated it to a special committee. This committee (which included Sherman but not Madison) proposed the "Connecticut" or "Grand" compromise that included proportional representation in the House and equal state representation in the Senate. After much more wrangling, the Convention adopted this solution on July 16.

The approval of this compromise on representation, in turn, instantly made some delegates recoil from the idea of broad national power. Madison understood from the first that the issues of representation and authority depended on one another. He believed that, if the large states and the rapidly growing Southern states enjoyed more voting power in the new Congress than in the Confederation, their "principal objections" to transferring power from the states to the national government would disappear.[38] Madison specifically predicted that the failure of proportional representation in the Senate would cause the Convention to withhold "every effectual prerogative" of national authority.[39] On the day the compromise was accepted, Randolph observed that "all the powers" proposed for the national government in the Virginia Plan "were founded on the supposition that a Proportional representation was to prevail in both branches of the Legislature."[40] The next day, Gouverneur Morris feared that equal representation in the Senate "would mix itself with the merits of every question concerning the powers."[41]

As he anticipated, some delegates who had supported Madison now began to advocate narrow national powers and extensive state authority. Southern delegates were especially worried about their ability to protect slavery. When the Convention revisited earlier language that authorized Congress to "legislate in all cases to which the separate States are incompetent; or in which the harmony of the U.S. may be interrupted by the exercise of individual legislation," South Carolina's John Rutledge called for a committee that would enumerate national powers, to constrict national authority and leave existing state prerogatives in place.[42] The next day, Sherman urged the Convention to approve a list of enumerated national powers and to prohibit the national government from interfering "with the Government of the individual States in any matters of internal police which respect the Government of such States only, and wherein the General welfare of the United States is not concerned."[43] When a Committee of Detail drafted a preliminary Constitution in early August, it dropped the Virginia Plan's broad warrant for national authority, specified a list of specific powers authorized for the national government, and added another list of powers that the states were not allowed to exercise.

This Committee of Detail report seemed to end all hope for broad national authority. The powers enumerated were written into the final Constitution.[44] For the rest of the Convention, proponents of broad nationalism had to fight to show that national authority on any specific issue should be expanded, and state authority diminished. While Madison sought to make the states prove that their powers did not harm the nation's interest, the Committee of Detail draft decisively placed the onus on the national government to prove that it required specific powers to pursue the national interest. States would retain prerogatives not granted to the national government.

Dividing Power

The delegates, then, designed American federalism by compromising on a series of disagreements about the specific powers of the national government. Narrow nationalism prevailed in protections for state power to tax, maintain a militia, and commercial power. Broad nationalism prevailed in new national taxing, military, and commercial authority, and in flexible powers that could be expanded in the future.

The Convention turned shared sovereignty from a theory into a reality when the delegates decided how to divide important government powers. Slavery was the foremost example. Southerners defended slavery more tenaciously as proportional representation in the Senate slipped away. Pierce Butler of South Carolina insisted that "The security the Southern States want is that their negroes may not be taken from them, which some gentlemen ... have a very good mind to do."[45] Narrowing national power and protecting state prerogatives could protect slavery. As Abraham Baldwin of Georgia put it, slavery, as "one of" Georgia's "favorite prerogatives," was an issue "of a local nature" that should be out of the reach of the national government.[46] Three provisions in the Constitution protected slavery in the Southern states. First, Southern delegates nailed down enough Southern seats in the House of Representatives to hamper any congressional move to do away with slavery. Three-fifths of the Southern slaves would be counted as part of the state population when it came time to allocate seats in the House of Representatives.[47] This three-fifths rule was a straightforward political compromise between Northern states, which did not want slaves counted at all (a formula that would increase Northern House seats), and Southern states, which wanted the slaves counted fully (thus increasing Southern House seats). Second, the Convention protected the slave trade by providing that Congress could not stop it until 1808, thus allowing South Carolina and Georgia to import slaves legally for a generation. Third, the Convention protected slavery by adding a "fugitive slave" clause, a provision that slaves who ran away from their owners—even across state lines and into the North—had to be returned.[48]

The delegates also narrowed national power by protecting most of the states' taxing, commercial, and military powers. Although the Constitution banned states from interfering in commerce by taxing imports and exports, they protected the states' power to levy other taxes. As Sherman put it, the states "retain a concurrent power of raising money for their own use."[49] Similarly, national authority over commerce included commerce with other nations and among the states, but not commerce *within* the states, which would remain under state authority. Further, the Constitution restricted national power to favor one region over others by requiring that all national commercial rules be uniform across the country.[50] The delegates refused to authorize additional specific national powers to encourage economic development, such as the power to charter corporations, construct canals, and establish a national university.[51] Finally, supporters of narrow nationalism largely shielded state militias from national control. Sherman argued that these militias were crucial: "the States might want their Militia for defense against invasions and insurrections, and for enforcing obedience to their laws. They will not give up this point."[52] Sherman complained that the idea of national appointment of top militia officers was "absolutely inadmissible."[53] In the final Constitution, the national government was required to get state permission even to intervene in internal state rebellions.

Though the supporters of narrow nationalism won key battles to protect important state powers, advocates of broad nationalism won many key points as well. Most important, they ensured that the Constitution authorized the national government to expand its power substantially. First, the Constitution firmly established that it and national laws "shall be the supreme Law of the Land," binding judges and overriding state laws where state and Federal law conflicted. The national courts would serve as watchdogs, defending national supremacy against state incursions. Second, the Committee of Detail gave the national government potentially broad authority to make all laws "necessary and proper" for executing all its enumerated powers.[54] The delegates did not contest this "necessary and proper" clause, because it seemed essential to give the national government some latitude. George Mason refused to sign the Constitution because he worried that provision allowed Congress to "extend their powers as far as they shall think proper; so that the State legislatures have no security for the powers now presumed to remain to them, or the people for their rights."[55] Third, a committee that considered proposals for additional national powers recommended more elastic language, expanding national authority "to provide, as may become necessary ... for the well managing and securing the common property and general interests and welfare of the United States," in a way that would not "interfere with the Governments of individual States in matters which respect only their internal Police, or for which their individual authorities may be competent."[56] The committee that wrote the final Constitution expanded this "general welfare" clause and dropped any protection for state powers. The preamble to the Constitution also reflected a vision of broad national government responsibility "to form a more perfect union, to establish justice, insure domestic tranquility, provide for the common defence, promote the general welfare, and secure the blessings of liberty to ourselves and our posterity."[57] The delegates did not contest this language.

The Constitution broadened national power by authorizing far-reaching military, taxing, and commercial authority for the U.S. government. Though the delegates protected the state militias, they refused to impose strict constraints on the national military, and defeated an effort to limit its size.[58] The national government would levy tariffs, and the delegates expected that these tariffs would provide a strong financial foundation for the government. The delegates also authorized a very broad national "power to lay and collect taxes, duties, imposts and excises."[59] The delegates refused to prohibit or put a time limit on the national government's power to levy direct taxes. To be sure, these direct taxes (such as taxes on property) had to be levied equally on a per capita basis, and this rule made it more difficult to design a national direct tax that met the Constitution's requirements.[60] But the restriction that direct taxes be applied per capita did not apply to national excise taxes, that is, taxes on specific goods (such as alcohol).[61] By the end of the Convention, even the most engaged delegates found it hard to understand the limits of the national taxing power.[62] Finally, the Constitution protected national commerce by limiting the states' powers to interfere in commerce among the states, by stabilizing currency, and by providing for more conservative regulation of credit.

Ratification and the Tenth Amendment

When the Convention delegates made their Constitution public, most returned to their states to fight for its ratification. Critics of the Constitution (the "Anti-Federalists") slammed the document for proposing so powerful a national government, warning that it would evolve into a centralized tyranny if the Constitution were approved. In their view, the strengthened national government would not accept competition from the states, but would soon consolidate power and swallow up the states. They repeated the conventional wisdom that sovereignty could not be shared, and criticized the Constitution for lacking safeguards such as a bill of rights to protect the states and the people.[63]

These criticisms forced leading delegates to further defend the notion of shared sovereignty and to show how the states would and could defend their prerogatives under the Constitution. Madison contributed the most thoughtful defense of state authority in his essays in the *Federalist*, published to advocate ratification in New York. Writing anonymously under the pen name "Publius," Madison assured readers that the states were "regarded as distinct and independent sovereigns" in the Constitution. He also assured them that

> The State Governments will have the advantage of the [F]ederal government, whether we compare them in respect to the immediate dependence of the one on the other; to the weight of personal influence which each side will possess; to the powers respectively vested in them; to the predilection and probable support of the people; to the disposition and faculty of resisting and frustrating the measures of each other.[64]

Madison noted that "the powers delegated by the proposed Constitution to the [F]ederal government, are few and defined. Those which are to remain in the State governments are numerous and indefinite."[65] Ellsworth, writing as "A Landholder," wrote that "State representation and government is the very basis of the congressional power proposed," and that the powers given placed "into the hands of your [F]ederal representatives," were general powers "such as must be exercised by the whole or not at all, and such as are absolutely necessary ... "[66]

Madison helped add the Bill of Rights to the Constitution, including the Tenth Amendment, another Constitutional defense for the states. When Virginia ratified the Constitution, it proposed an additional list of guarantees against national power, including a rule "that each state in the Union shall respectively retain every power, jurisdiction, and right, which is not by this Constitution delegated to the Congress of the United States, or to the departments of the [F]ederal government."[67] Madison promised the Virginia voters who elected him to the first House of Representatives that he would propose a similar bill of rights, and he did so a month after the new Congress began its session. Madison's list of rights included a version of the protection for the states, and his suggestion became the Tenth Amendment: "The powers not delegated to the United States by the Constitution, nor prohibited by it to the States, are reserved to the States respectively, or to the people." This amendment seemed to strengthen the case that the national government bore the burden of proof for exercising any authority not enumerated in the Constitution. But the Tenth Amendment provides no guidance about the precise boundary between state and national power. Madison himself did not think this amendment was necessary at all.[68] Subsequently, opponents of expanded Federal power have used other provisions of the Constitution, rather than the Tenth Amendment, as the basis of their arguments.[69] The Tenth Amendment, then, did little to settle but much to encourage conflicts over the legitimate authority of the national and state governments.

The Constitution of Power in American Federalism

While many ideas and philosophies shaped the framers' notions of federalism, the specific Constitutional provisions that established the foundations of American federalism, then, were the product of power struggles at the Constitutional Convention.[70] More than anything else, the delegates aimed to build governing institutions that would shape the use and pursuit of power in the future. They knew these institutions would, in turn, create opportunities for those Americans who wanted to pursue and use government power. Because a series of ingenious and expedient compromises produced American federalism, it is futile to try to find a single, logical blueprint for federalism in the Convention debates or the Constitution. In the end, advocates of both broad and narrow nationalism could claim some success in its design, because they had created a government that was "partly federal, partly national." Madison described this new form of federalism as "compound republic" in the *Federalist*.[71]

The key to understanding the original design of this compound republic lies in the way it distributed the tools of government power between the states and the national, or as it quickly became known, the Federal government. American federalism distributed the tools of everyday governing to the states, allocated the tools of sovereignty to the national government, injected state interests into national politics and policy-making, and created a double political battleground in American politics.

States' Powers: The Tools of Everyday Governing and their Limits

First, the Constitution allowed the states to keep the powers of everyday governing, that is, to retain most of the policy tools for governing everyday American life. During the ratification debates, "A Freeman," writing in support of the Constitution, pointed out how extensive these tools were. States would retain power over taxes (except on imports or exports), militias, criminal law, property, and contracts, "corporations civil and religious," and the creation of cities, counties, courts, schools, "poor houses, hospitals, and houses of employment." They could regulate vices, manage politics and elections (including elections to national office), promote their own manufactures, and build roads and canals.[72] Within their borders, then, the state governments had power over labor (including slave labor), capital, land, natural resources, and energy—all the basic elements of a productive economy. With the blessing of the Constitution, then, the individual state republics had the power to manage and nurture the growth of social relationships, their economies, and their politics.

The states' powers in the compound republic, in turn, profoundly shaped every major step in American political development. Most of the major public policy conflicts of American history, whether over race, economic development, political reform, social welfare, education, health, the environment, or dozens of other explosive issues, initially have been fought out at the state and local level because states had the power to deal with them. Since each state had different resources, cultures, histories, and many other qualities, each state has done things differently. The power to make policy is the power to do things differently. As political scientist Aaron Wildavsky wrote, federalism is all about inequality: the encouragement of diversity "lies at the heart of federalism. ... It is inequality of result, not merely in income (some states choosing high tax, high services, others the opposite) but also in lifestyle, that distinguishes federalism as a living system from federalism as a front for a unitary power."[73] Thus some states apply capital punishment for crimes, or discourage trade union organization, or ban gay marriage, while others do not. American public policy is fragmented and varied as a result of this state power.

Moreover, because the states lacked the full set of powers that sovereign national governments always have used to respond to these conflicts, state policies have been more limited than policies abroad. The Constitution amputated important powers of sovereignty that nation-states could use. These policy tools included printing money, taxing imports, and restricting trade. Immediately after the Convention ended, Sherman and Ellsworth explained how these clauses worked together to protect free markets:

> The restraint on the legislatures of the several states respecting emitting bills of credit, making any thing but money a tender in payment of debts, or impairing the obligation of contracts by ex post facto laws, was thought necessary as a security to commerce, in which the interest of foreigners, as well as of the citizens of different states, may be affected.[74]

National governments have used these powers to balance the costs and benefits of national policy. These tools also can delay, shift, or even conceal the adverse impacts of public policy. American states were denied a full toolbox of policy instruments, and without them, states—the principal economic policy-makers for most of American history—found that any policy that harmed businesses or interfered with markets had much more immediate, visible, and politically costly effects than the same policies enacted by a national government that could make use of the full range of economic tools. The Constitution exposed each state to national market competition from enterprises in other states, and it largely prohibited each state from inhibiting the expansion of the American market economy. State policy-makers, then, came under strong pressures to help private enterprise and facilitate market-driven economic growth. Businesses quickly and routinely complain about any regulation or tax that seems to disadvantage them in national competition. Sometimes, these businesses threaten to move to other states with more favorable policies. From the beginning, then, the short-term interests of entrepreneurs and speculators weighed very heavily in most state decisions about taxes, business regulations, land use, and natural resources.[75]

National Power: The Powers of National Sovereignty and their Limits

Second, the Constitution authorized the national government to exercise the powers of national sovereignty, that is, the tools of diplomacy, commerce, and national security exercised by other sovereign national governments. The Federal government could go to war, build alliances, and manage trade to the advantage of the nation. But the Constitution did not give the national government the full toolbox of policy powers needed for managing the development of the nation, its politics, and its economy. States, not the national government, had and kept the power to govern their own culture, politics, and economy. Because Federal policy-makers lacked the authority to regulate everyday life, they gradually learned to use Federal revenues as an instrument for exercising a limited measure of national action. Federal grants-in-aid to the states aimed to induce state governments across the nation to undertake new policy activities in specific fields (see Chapters 6 and 7).

The compound republic also made political cooperation difficult to build and maintain across the whole nation. The Constitution's framers deliberately infused federalism thoroughly into the institutions of national policy-making. The delegates built a national policy process that assumed and encouraged robust republican politics organized around state and local interests. National institutions supported different, sometimes conflicting policies because they represented different geographical interests in different ways. The U.S. House of Representatives, elected every two years, constructs public policy around a majority of relatively short-term, sub-regional interests. The U.S. Senate, elected by states for six-year terms, constructs public policy around a majority of state interests. Only an extraordinarily large geographical majority could win approval in both the House and Senate for any public policy measure. No law could be passed in the 1st Congress without, at a bare minimum, the consent of representatives of fifty-five percent of the American population.[76] Additionally, the state-based Senate plays a larger role in governing than the House because it alone approves treaties and presidential appointments. The Constitution, then, created a complicated national government that protected the delegates' diverse state constituencies by filling the policy process with potential veto points: the Senate and House effectively could veto each other, and the president could veto any bill on which they could agree.

The Unsettled Boundary of Government Powers

Third, the unsettled dividing line between state and national power animated substantive political struggles throughout American history. The politicians who negotiated American federalism deliberately left the power-sharing details blurry and the line between state and national authority imprecise. They left the ensuing boundary disputes for future politicians to work through. The framers of the Constitution therefore built enduring conflict over federalism into the government by authorizing both the states and the national government to expand future policy and by leaving the boundary between state and national authority so ambiguous. Madison expected such conflicts, and in the *Federalist* essays, he celebrated this potential conflict as a check on national power.

> In a single republic, all the power surrendered by the people is submitted to the administration of a single government; and the usurpations are guarded against by a division of the government into distinct and separate departments. In the compound republic of America, the power surrendered by the people is first divided between two distinct governments, and then the portion allotted to each subdivided among distinct and separate departments. Hence a double security arises to the rights of the people. The different governments will control each other, at the same time that each will be controlled by itself.[77]

Here, Madison argues that the states can check the national exercise of power, and invites them to do so. This ambiguity, combined with the provision that states would exercise powers not specifically granted to Congress, "amounted to a standing invitation to contest the [F]ederal government's power," according to historian Ronald P. Formisano.[78] "The political logic of federalism," concludes legal historian Herbert Wechsler, "thus supports placing the burden of persuasion on those urging national action."[79]

The Double Battleground of American Politics

Fourth, this unsettled frontier of power, combined with political conflict over the control of power, turned American federalism into an arena of political conflict. The Constitution's prestige as the nation's source of fundamental law, combined with its ambiguity, has made federalism an irresistible battleground in American political conflict because it gives political adversaries the incentive and the opportunity to use the Constitution as a shield and a sword. Those who oppose more national power to deal with a particular problem often have invoked specific constitutional provisions as a shield against interference with state prerogatives, as has often happened in racial or economic development disputes in

American history. Those who want change often invoke national supremacy and elastic power as a sword to establish national prerogatives against the states.

These contested provisions have divided and complicated American government and politics by creating a double battleground. The first battleground—the political battleground that exists in every nation—involves whether the government should act to deal with a public problem or not. In every nation, many fundamental political battles are fought over whether the government should do something about health, welfare, the economy, morals, or any of the thousands of specific situations that some define as a public problem deserving government attention. But the second battleground turns on which level of government should have the power to choose whether to act. As the following chapters make clear, this second alternative has had a far-reaching impact on the nation's evolution.

The Framers' Legacy

The Constitution's framers created a resilient republic that has endured wrenching social change, economic catastrophe, war, and extraordinary growth. This resilient republic was a political compound: the Federal government had the authority to lead the nation into its future, while the states kept the authority to maintain most of the governing arrangements that existed when the Constitutional Convention met. Advocates of narrow nationalism won a limited, enumerated list of national powers, state control of substantial policy authority, and political weapons that states could use to fight the unwanted aggregation of national power. Advocates of broad nationalism won some explicit new national powers with elastic potential, a Constitutional guarantee that national law would be supreme, and Constitutional language that could be used to expand national power on a case-by-case basis.

A century later, Woodrow Wilson explained the Constitution's unfinished framework of federalism shaped the development of America fundamentally.

> The question of the relation of the states to the [F]ederal government is the cardinal question of our constitutional system ... It cannot, indeed, be settled by the opinion of any one generation because it is a question of growth, and every successive stage of our political and economic development gives it a new aspect.[80]

Meanwhile, Americans were forging this unfinished Constitutional framework into a set of weapons for conducting political warfare.

Notes

1. Lawrence M. Friedman, *A History of American Law*, 3rd ed. (New York: Touchstone, 2005), 3–53; Robert A. Becker, *Revolution, Reform, and the Politics of American Taxation, 1763–1783* (Baton Rouge, LA: Louisiana State University Press, 1980); Albert Anthony Giesecke, *American Commercial Legislation before 1789* (New York: Burt Franklin, 1970 [orig. 1910]); Margaret Ellen Newell, "The Birth of New England in the Atlantic Economy: From Its Beginning to 1770," in *Engines of Enterprise: An Economic History of New England*, ed. Peter Temin (Cambridge, MA: Harvard University Press, 2000), 41; Gordon S. Wood, *The Creation of the American Republic, 1776–1787* (Chapel Hill, NC: University of North Carolina Press, 1969), 166–67; Peter C. Ordeshook and Olga Shvetsova, "Federalism and Constitutional Design," *Journal of Democracy* 8:1 (January, 1997), 27–42.

2. Joseph L. Davis, *Sectionalism in American Politics, 1774–1787* (Madison, WI: University of Wisconsin Press, 1977), 16–19; Gary M. Walton and Hugh Rockoff, *History of the American Economy*, 8th ed. (Fort Worth, TX: Dryden Press, 1998), 94–113, 147–50.

3. See comments by Alexander Hamilton, in *The Records of the Federal Convention of 1787* [hereafter, *RFC*], ed. Max Farrand, 4 vols. (New Haven, CT: Yale University Press, 1937), June 29, I, 466, and James Madison, *RFC*, June 30, I, 486–87.

4. Curtis P. Nettels, *The Emergence of a National Economy, 1775–1815* (New York: Holt, Rinehart, and Winston, 1962), 138, 146; Allan Nevins, *The American States during and after the Revolution, 1775–1789* (New York: Macmillan, 1924), 598; Forrest McDonald, *Novus Ordo Seclorum: The Intellectual Origins of the Constitution* (Lawrence, KS: University Press of Kansas, 1985), 217–19; Gary M. Walton and James F. Shepard, *The Economic Rise of Early America* (New York: Cambridge University Press, 1979), 102.

5. Nettels, *The Emergence of a National Economy*, 75–81, 86; Jackson Turner Main, *The Sovereign States, 1775–1783* (New York: New Viewpoints, 1973), 235; David P. Szatmary, *Shay's Rebellion: The Making of an American Insurrection* (Amherst, MA: University of Massachusetts Press, 1980); James Ferguson, *The Power of the Purse: A History of Public Finance, 1776–1790* (Chapel Hill, NC: University of North Carolina Press, 1961), 243–49; Roger H. Brown, *Redeeming the Republic: Federalists, Taxation, and the Origins of the Constitution* (Baltimore, MD: Johns Hopkins University Press, 1993), 83–96, 108–21; Leonard L. Richards, *Shays's Rebellion: The American Revolution's Final Battle* (Philadelphia, PA: University of Pennsylvania Press, 2003).

6. William Pierce to George Turner, May 19, 1787, in *Supplement to Max Farrand's The Records of the Federal Convention of 1787*, ed. James L. Hutson (New Haven, CT: Yale University Press, 1987), 10; Jack N. Rakove, *Original Meanings: Politics and Ideas in the Making of the Constitution* (New York: Alfred A. Knopf, 1996), 33.

7. George Washington to David Stuart, July 1, 1787, *RFC* III, 51–52.

8. David Brian Robertson, *The Constitution and America's Destiny* (Cambridge and New York: Cambridge University Press, 2005), 68–71.

9. Rakove, *Original Meanings*, 31–34; Richard Beeman, *Plain, Honest Men: The Making of the American Constitution* (New York: Random House, 2009).

10. Clinton Rossiter, *1787: The Grand Convention* (New York: Macmillan, 1966), 79–156.

11. James H. Charleton and Robert G. Ferris, eds., *Framers of the Constitution* (Washington, DC: Smithsonian Institution Press, 1986); U.S. Congress, *Biographical Directory of the United States Congress, 1774–1989* (Washington, DC: Government Printing Office, 1989).

12. Ralph Ketcham, *James Madison: A Biography* (Charlottesville, VA: University Press of Virginia, 1971).

13. James Madison, "Vices of the Political System of the United States," in *The Papers of James Madison*, ed. William T. Hutchinson et al., 17 vols. (Chicago: University of Chicago Press, 1975), 9: 348–54; see Richard K. Matthews, *If Men were Angels: James Madison and the Heartless Empire of Reason* (Lawrence, KS: University Press of Kansas, 1995), 178–84.

14. *RFC*, June 7, I, 154.

15. *RFC*, June 28, I, 449.

16. David Brian Robertson, "Madison's Opponents and Constitutional Design," *American Political Science Review* 99:2 (May, 2005), 227–28.

17. *RFC*, June 8, I, 164–65.

18. *RFC*, May 29, I, 20–22.

19. *RFC*, July 5, I, 530.

20. *RFC*, June 18, I, 287.

21. *RFC*, June 8, I, 164.

22. *RFC*, June 30, I, 484–85; July 2, I, 510–11.

23. *RFC*, June 8, I, 167.

24. *RFC*, June 29, I, 461.

25. *Supplement to Max Farrand's The Records of the Federal Convention of 1787*, June 25, 112–13.

26. *RFC*, June 30, I, 492.

27. Wood, *The Creation of the American Republic, 1776–1787*, 527–28; Rakove, *Original Meanings*, 182–84, 188–89.

28. *RFC*, June 18, I, 287.

29. *RFC*, June 8, I, 172.

30. *RFC*, June 29, I, 467.

31. *RFC*, June 6, I, 133.

32. *RFC*, June 16, I, 251.

33. *RFC*, June 7, 1, 152–55.

34. *RFC*, June 21, I, 355.

35. *RFC*, June 25, I, 416.

36. *RFC*, June 29, I, 468–69.

37. *RFC*, July 2, I, 511.

38. Madison to George Washington, April 16, 1787, in *The Papers of James Madison* 9: 383.

39. *RFC*, July 6, I, 551.

40. *RFC*, June 16, I, 17.

41. *RFC*, July 17, II, 25.

42. *RFC*, July 16, II, 17.

43. *RFC*, July 17, II, 25–26.

44. *RFC*, August 8, II, 220.

45. *RFC*, July 13, I, 605.

46. *RFC*, August 22, II, 372.

47. *RFC*, July 12, I, 595–96.

48. *RFC*, August 21, II, 363–64.

49. *RFC*, August 18, II, 332.

50. *RFC*, August 28, II, 437–38.

51. *RFC*, August 18, II, 325.

52. *RFC*, August 18, II, 332–33.

53. *RFC*, August 23, II, 388.

54. *RFC*, August 6, II, 181–83, 187.

55. *RFC*, September 15, II, 640.

56. *RFC*, August 22, II, 367.

57. Compare *RFC*, II, 569 and II, 594. The preamble is at II, 590.

58. *RFC*, August 18, II, 330; September 5, II, 508.

59. *RFC*, August 6, I, 181; August 16, II, 308.

60. *RFC*, September 14, II, 618.

61. *RFC*, August 20, II, 350; August 21, II, 355–56; August 22, II, 366–67.

62. *RFC*, September 15, II, 625.

63. Rakove, *Original Meanings*, 181–88.

64. James Madison, *Federalist* 40 and *Federalist* 45, in Alexander Hamilton, James Madison, and John Jay, *The Federalist*, ed. Jacob E. Cooke (Middletown, CT: Wesleyan University Press, 1961), 261, 311.

65. Madison, *Federalist* 45, 313.

66. "A Landholder" (Oliver Ellsworth), IV, November 26, 1787, http://teachingamericanhistory.org/library/index.asp?documentprint=1653 (accessed January 2, 2010).

67. Virginia Ratifying Convention, "Proposed Amendments to the Constitution 27 June 1788" in Jonathan Elliot, ed., *The Debates in the Several State Conventions on the Adoption of the Federal Constitution* (New York: Burt Franklin, 1968) 3:657.

68. U.S. House of Representatives, Debates on Amendments to the Constitution, in *The Founders' Constitution*, Vol. 5, *Bill of Rights*, Document 11, http://press-pubs.uchicago.edu/founders/documents/bill_of_rightss11.html (accessed December 15, 2009).

69. John F. Manning "Federalism and the Generality Problem in Constitutional Interpretation," *Harvard Law Review* 122:8 (June, 2009), 2003–69.

70. On the ideas that shaped federalism, see Alison LaCroix, *The Ideological Origins of American Federalism*, (Cambridge, MA: Harvard University Press, 2010).

71. Madison, *Federalist* 51, 351, and *Federalist* 62, 416.

72. "A Freeman" (Tench Cox), II, January 30, 1788, *The Online Library of Liberty*, http://oll.libertyfund.org/?option=com_staticxt&staticfile=show.php%3Ftitle=2069&chapter=156158&layout=html&Itemid=27 (accessed July 7, 2010).

73. Aaron Wildavsky, "Federalism is about Inequality," in *The Costs of Federalism*, eds. Robert T. Golembiewski and Aaron Wildavsky (New Brunswick, NJ: Transaction Books, 1984), 66.

74. Roger Sherman and Oliver Ellsworth to the Governor of Connecticut, letter, September 26, 1787, *RFC* III, 100.

75. Harry N. Scheiber, "Federalism and the American Economic Order, 1789–1910," *Law and Society Review* 10:1 (Fall, 1975), 57–118.

76. For example, a minimum winning coalition of New England and the Middle states would require New Hampshire (with three Representatives and two Senators), Massachusetts (eight Representatives and two Senators), Connecticut (five Representatives and two Senators), New York (five Representatives and two Senators), New Jersey (four Representatives and two Senators), and Pennsylvania (eight Representatives and two Senators), and a Senator from another state, either Rhode Island or Delaware (each with two Senators but only one Representative). This coalition of states would represent fifty-four percent of the House of Representatives, fifty-five percent of the population of the thirteen states according to the 1790 census, and fifty-six percent of the October, 1786 Confederation requisition. A minimum winning coalition that included all the large states would require the unanimous support of Representatives from Virginia (ten Representatives), Pennsylvania (eight), and Massachusetts (eight) and, for example, Maryland (six) and the three states with the smallest representation: Georgia (three), Delaware (one), and Rhode Island (one). This coalition represented about fifty-seven percent of the House of Representatives and of the population of the thirteen states according to the 1790 census.

77. Madison, *Federalist* 51, 350–51.

78. Ronald P. Formisano, "State Development in the Early Republic: Substance and Structure, 1780–1840," in *Contesting Democracy: Substance and Structure in American Political History*, eds. Byron E. Shafer and Anthony Badger (Lawrence, KS: University Press of Kansas, 2001), 11.

79. Herbert Wechsler, "The Political Safeguards of Federalism: The Role of the States in the Composition and Selection of the National Government," *Columbia Law Review* 54:4 (April 1954), 545.

80. Woodrow Wilson, *Constitutional Government in the United States* (New York: Columbia University Press, 1908), 173.

Reading 1.2

Functions of Courts, Basics of Legal Analysis, and Sources of Law

Mark C. Miller

T HE STUDY OF AMERICAN JUDICIAL POLITICS involves examining how courts, judges, and other judicial actors function and interact in the U.S. political system. For a long time, scholars studying the courts tended to treat them as a unique branch of the government, and judicial scholars tended to focus solely on the judiciary. Today, however, more and more scholars are studying the courts not as isolated institutions but instead as vital parts of the larger integrated political system. Scholars are now looking at how judges and courts interact with the other branches of government and with the general public. They are also studying how American judges interact with their colleagues abroad. Thus, courts are now seen as a part of the broader system of government in a world transformed by globalization.

Courts are generally becoming more important and increasing their power around the globe.[1] After World War II, many countries created new constitutional courts or greatly strengthened existing ones.[2] For example, the European Court of Justice became a highly activist court interpreting and enforcing European law throughout the member states of the European Union.[3] However, American courts have remained some of the most powerful courts in the world. Summing up the views of most judicial politics scholars around the globe, Martin Shapiro, a prominent political scientist, wrote, "If any nation is the peculiar home of the expansion of judicial power, it is the United States."[4] Therefore, it seems natural that the study of judicial politics started with the political study of courts and law in the United States before spreading into the study of judicial systems around the world. This book will focus on judicial politics in the United States, although it will make comparisons to other countries when appropriate.

Judicial Politics Defined

Before we define judicial politics, we should start at the beginning—with a definition of **law**. *Black's Law Dictionary* states that laws are "rules promulgated by government as a means to an ordered society." (Note that terms in **bold** are defined in the Glossary, found at the end of the book.) Another standard dictionary definition states that laws are "the principles and regulations established by a government or other authority and applicable to a people, whether by legislation or by custom, enforced by judicial decision." Some political scientists define law as "[t]he presence of a centralized authority capable of exacting coercive penalties for violations of legal rules."[5] And according to many sociologists, "[l]aws are rules that are enforced and sanctioned by the authority of government."[6] In short, law is a system of ideas and rules, while the U.S. courts are the human and political institutions that interpret the law. Thus, courts use the law in order to do justice. Obviously, the rule of law and the role of courts go hand in hand.

The law is often described as having its own language and its own analytical approach. Since law is a closed system of rules, legal reasoning in part means understanding, and carefully using, the unique meaning of words in the law, which can differ greatly from their meaning in regular English usage. One of the keys to legal reasoning is "thinking like a lawyer," which means speaking, writing, and reading like a lawyer or a judge.[7] Legal reasoning is an analytical approach that pays special attention to the specific legal use of language as well as to the rules of society. Therefore, the law is in large part the language that lawyers and judges use when they resolve human conflicts using the official rules made by the government.[8]

Laws usually also reflect the norms of a particular society or group. **Norms** are less official than laws and can be defined as "shared rules of conduct that specify how people ought to think and act."[9] The violation of social norms may cause some discomfort for an individual, but the violation of laws may lead to formal legal penalties imposed by the judiciary as representatives of the society. Therefore, law is an approach to dispute resolution that works to preserve social peace and order, and it incorporates both the legal rules and the collective norms of a society.[10]

Next, we need a definition of politics. **Politics** is generally the allocation of power and resources in a society. According to Harold Lasswell, a famous political scientist, "Politics is who gets what, when, and how."[11] Politics obviously deals with the workings of government and includes issues concerning how priorities, costs, and benefits are distributed in a society. As David Easton, another political scientist, argued, "Politics is the authoritative allocation of values."[12] Politics can involve individuals, interest groups, and political parties, and all of these are important in their relationship to the courts. Laws are the end product of politics and are "the prize over which many political struggles have been waged."[13] Thus, law and politics are closely related.

The academic study of the combination of law and politics is known as **judicial politics**, which is often defined as "the political process by which courts are constituted and legal decisions are made and implemented."[14] Sociolegal scholars come from a variety of academic disciplines, but most scholars of judicial politics have their home in the field of political science. Political scientists tend to study the courts as a political institution as well as a legal institution.

Notice that the term *judicial politics* assumes that judges in the United States are both legal and political actors at the same time, making their decisions in part based on legal reasoning and legal analysis and in part based on ideology and other political factors. In the United States, courts are policy makers, just like legislative and executive officials. This is how one group of political scientists describes the intersection of law and politics: "Modern political systems rely on law as one of *the* chief instruments, if not *the* chief instrument, to carry out national objectives and distribute rights and duties. Thus courts and judges, insofar as they help to determine and apply 'the law,' are inevitably participants in the political processes."[15]

The study of judicial politics also includes how courts and judges interact with other political actors and institutions, including interest groups, the media, Congress, the president, the federal bureaucracy, and of course the general public. This book will explore all of these aspects of judicial politics in the United States.

Scholars might argue that, in many parts of the world, law and politics are two distinct realms and ideas, although most political scientists feel that the separation between these two concepts is an artificial one, even abroad.[16] But in the United States, law and politics have clearly been closely intertwined since our nation's founding.[17] It was no accident that lawyers were very influential among the writers of the Declaration of Independence of 1776 and the Constitution of 1789. A little less than half of the signers of the Declaration of Independence were lawyers, and lawyers constituted more than half of the attendees at the Constitutional Convention. Lawyers also dominated the state conventions called to ratify the U.S. Constitution and the conventions called to write the original state constitutions after the American Revolution.[18] It is no accident that the United States has historically had one of the highest proportions of lawyer-legislators in the world.[19] Lawyers are also elected in large numbers to be presidents of the United States and governors of the fifty states.[20] John Adams was the first of many lawyer-presidents, and he always felt that law should be thought of in combination with other great ideas, including politics, philosophy, and jurisprudence.[21]

In the United States, courts make legal decisions, but they also create public policy in a wide variety of areas, including free speech rights, abortion rights, the rights of criminal defendants, rules for drawing the lines of legislative districts, and the issue of spoken prayer in public schools, among many others. In most other societies, these public policy decisions would be made by the national legislative body or by the bureaucracy.[22] However, in the United States law has never been isolated from political considerations.

Alexis de Tocqueville, a French philosopher, traveled to the United States in the early 1800s in order to compare American society and politics to the European models with which he was most familiar, in particular those of France and England. Tocqueville was fascinated with the role of lawyers and judges in the United States, arguing among other things that lawyers constituted the American aristocracy and noting that American judges were more powerful than jurists anywhere else in the world. He also observed that in America all legal issues eventually become political ones and all political issues eventually become legal ones. As Tocqueville wrote in his book *Democracy in America*, "The judicial organization of the United States is the hardest thing there for a foreigner to understand. He finds judicial authority invoked in almost every political context, and from that he naturally concludes that the judge is one of the most important political powers in the United States."[23]

Our Common Law Roots

The mixture of law and politics in the United States has roots in our historical connections to Great Britain. When the British founded the American colonies that eventually became the United States, they brought their notion of law and legal reasoning with them. Therefore, American courts and the broader American judicial system are part of the international Anglo-American common law family of legal systems. The **common law** family of legal systems originated in England and is based on judge-made court decisions and legal **precedent**, or the articulation of legal principles in a historical succession of judicial decisions, rather than on codified written laws, as in some other legal traditions. In short, in the United States, a court's ruling today is based in large part on the rulings of past judges on similar legal issues. The precedent of prior judicial rulings, referred to with the Latin term *stare decisis* (almost literally "let the ruling stand"), is quite fundamental in common law countries.

Anglo-American judges decide current cases and disputes using the reasoning of prior similar cases as their foundation. In addition, judges on lower courts must follow the precedents of higher courts in our legal system. This concept is often called **binding precedent**, which means that the lower court judges must follow the rulings of higher courts in their court hierarchy. By contrast, **persuasive precedent** means that judges may, but are not required to, borrow the reasoning used by judges on roughly equivalent courts. Another way to put this is that binding precedent is a vertical type of precedent, while persuasive precedent is a horizontal type of precedent. For example, persuasive precedent often occurs when one state supreme court borrows the approach of another state supreme court, even though it is not required to do so.

The Anglo-American common law approach clearly has its roots in the English legal tradition. The English developed a system of professionalized judges very early after the Norman Conquest in 1066, and the king sent these professional judges out into the countryside to make legal decisions in his name. These judges helped resolve disputes that the king did not have the time or the desire to adjudicate. They often incorporated local norms into their decisions, but not all local or regional customs became commonly accepted throughout the kingdom. In order to remember why they had ruled as they did in prior cases, the king's judges began to write down the reasoning for their decisions. The written collective reasoning and rulings of these professional judges (precedent) thus eventually became the common law of the English kingdom. Common law rules evolved as judges used precedent from other judges' decisions blended with local customs as the foundations for their judicial rulings.[24] Thus, the Anglo-American common law principles evolved over time, instead of being enacted in a single comprehensive legal code written by legal experts, as happened in ancient Rome or in Napoleon's France, for example. The common law is thus often considered judge-made law. The judge's job in a common law system is to do justice in the particular case before him or her.

Today, common law judges are drawn strictly from the legal profession, and thus judges must first work as lawyers before they can be elevated to the bench. In many other societies, lawyers and judges are seen as two distinct professions with separate educational requirements, and individuals are unable to move from one profession to the other. In the common law world, however, judging and lawyering are closely linked, with relatively frequent movement between the two spheres of what is really considered a single profession. Because professional judges come from the ranks of attorneys and are trained to use precedent as the foundation for their decision making, in the common law tradition only one judge is needed per case at the trial level. However, in the appellate courts, panels of multiple judges hear appeals in this legal system.

Differences between the Common Law and Civil Law Traditions

The common law tradition developed first in England soon after the Norman Conquest and later spread throughout the entire English-speaking world. This tradition is much different from the **civil law** family of legal systems of Continental Europe that are based on the Roman and Napoleonic written legal codes, with France, Spain, and Germany probably being the most notable contemporary models.[25] These civil law legal systems have spread into Japan, Latin America, Eastern Europe, and parts of Asia, among other places.[26] This section will compare various aspects of the common law legal systems with those in the civil law tradition.

One of the key differences between the two legal traditions is that in the common law tradition, judges are aided by an **adversary system**, that is, a system where lawyers protect the interests of their clients and present their clients' best case to the court. From the clash of these two opposing sides in the adversary system, the judge or jury should be able to determine the just result in any particular case. Common law courts worry much more about doing justice than they do about finding the one right legal answer or even the truth in a specific case. On the other hand, in an inquisitorial civil law system, the lawyers, judges, and prosecutors in theory all work together to find the singular truth. As mentioned earlier in the chapter, the law in the common law world is constantly evolving as judges face new situations and must apply the law to ever changing social realities. However, changes in the law in the civil law tradition come only from the national legislatures. Judges in the civil law world merely apply the legal code to the facts before them, but they never make law in the way common law judges can and often do. In the civil law systems, law is generally created by legal experts who write a nation's detailed comprehensive legal code. These complex legal codes with their interlocking rules are then enacted into law by the country's national legislative bodies. These codes are comprehensive, and in theory civil law judges cannot add to the codes or fill in the gaps—they merely apply the code to the specific set of facts before them.

In the civil law tradition, law should be uniform throughout the nation. In the common law world, however, local variations in the law are much more acceptable and happen fairly often. This is in large part because the common law legal systems do not employ a single comprehensive legal code; instead, common law judges use multiple sources of law such as constitutional provisions, statutes, bureaucratic decisions, and perhaps multiple judicial precedents in order to find a just result in any given case. In fact, in many countries that are part of the common law tradition, it was well into the nineteenth century before their national parliaments began enacting statutes that dealt with the everyday lives of common citizens.[27]

In civil law countries, judges do not normally use the concept of precedent. They would merely apply the national code to the case at hand, without examining prior judicial decisions.[28] Because of the fear that a single judge might apply the legal code incorrectly, trial courts in the civil law tradition almost always use at least three judges to hear a case. Very few civil law countries use juries in their trials, but lay trial juries are quite prevalent in the common law world. The sole purpose of civil law appellate courts is to correct any errors committed at trial. Also, appeals courts are much more likely to hear a case *de novo* (starting over from the beginning, almost like a second trial) in civil law countries than they are in common law nations. In common law systems, appeals courts tend to focus as much on creating the right precedent as they do on correcting errors.

In the common law world, law can be seen as an art, where different judges may come to different conclusions on what is a just result in any given case. This is in part because judges must utilize and interpret multiple sources of law and perhaps multiple precedents. In the civil law world, one may think of law as a science, where the job of the judge is to find the one right answer using a single source of law (the legal code). While the key figure in the common law world is the creative and innovative judge in search of justice, in the civil law world the primary source of law is the careful and diligent legal scholar who writes the lucid, detailed, and all-encompassing legal codes that are then enacted into law by the national legislature.[29]

General Theories of Law

In our common law system, there are several general theories of law that judges might use in their decision making. These theories reflect the fact that there are basically two views of the law among legal scholars in our country. Some believe that the law is inherently based on some underlying and universal moral standard, while others hold that it is merely the product of social construction.[30] These two approaches can be called natural law theories and positive law theories, respectively.

Natural law theories propose that there are universal rules and norms that supersede laws created by individuals. Since natural law is a higher form of law, lesser human-made laws must yield to the dictates of natural law.[31] Another way of stating this is that natural law looks to "unquestioned universal principles" that inspire and yet subsume legal texts written by human individuals.[32] Some have argued that Justice Clarence Thomas retains elements of natural law theory in many of his judicial opinions.[33]

There are generally three streams of natural law theory: religious, rational, and historical. The religious stream of natural law argues that law is divinely given by God or other higher being. In particular, Catholic natural law theories often find their roots in the thinking of St. Thomas Aquinas, a theologian and philosopher from the thirteenth century. The rational stream of natural law stresses that there are universal rules for human behavior that only rational thought can discover. Influenced by seventeenth- and eighteenth-century Enlightenment thinkers who stressed the importance of observation and experiment in arriving at reliable and demonstrable universal truths, rationalist secular natural law elevates the capacity of the human intellect over the spiritual authority of religion. The third approach, the historical stream, relies on the customs and traditions of civilized societies in order to establish universal rules of behavior. According to these thinkers, law must be made to conform to the well-established but usually unwritten customs, traditions, and experiences that have evolved over the course of history.

In contrast to these natural law theories, **positive law theories** often argue that law should reflect the will of a majority in a society. Thus, the law should be whatever the majority of citizens say it is, as determined through majoritarian democratic processes. Moral concerns play no role in positive theories of the law.

A third approach to the law is more sociological. **Sociological theories of law** often argue that law "represents a reflection of the values, mores, and culture of the society that produces it."[34] As a society changes, the law will change as well. Political scientists tend to study the political effects of law because they usually see law and politics as inherently intertwined. Thus, political scientists tend to adopt the thinking that laws are whatever the majority of a society enacts through the political and governmental processes.

Sources of Law in the United States

Like all common law courts, courts in the United States interpret a variety of sources of law. In the United States, there is a clear hierarchy of sources of law that judges can use. Figure 1.2.1 lists the American sources of law in order of hierarchy. Anything higher in the hierarchy can generally overrule any lower source of law. At the top of the hierarchy is the highest source of law in the United States, the U.S. Constitution, which the courts interpret through their power of judicial review (defined in more detail on page 14). The next category of sources of law includes federal statutes, joint resolutions, and treaties. **Federal statutes** are laws enacted by the U.S. Congress and either signed into law by the president or under certain circumstances allowed to become law without his signature. If the president vetoes a proposed law passed by Congress, it nevertheless becomes a statute if two-thirds of both houses of Congress vote to override the president's veto. In some limited circumstances, joint resolutions serve the same function as bills in Congress. Federal **treaties** are agreements between nations that are negotiated by the president and ratified by a two-thirds vote of the U.S. Senate. Many societies consider treaties as superior to their national constitutions (for example, the member states of the European Union do this), but in the United States treaties are treated as inferior to the U.S. Constitution. However, treaties are usually considered on the same level as federal statutes because normally the U.S. Congress must enact a variety of measures in order to implement any given treaty.

The next source of law is **presidential executive orders**, usually directed at executive branch agencies in the permanent federal bureaucracy.[35] The president has the power to issue executive orders to the agencies, directing them to do, or refrain from doing, certain things.[36] Following this are **federal agency rules and regulations,** which are the adjudicatory decisions an agency uses to enforce its regulations against various actors within the

1. U.S. Constitution
    ↓
2. Federal statutes, joint resolutions, and treaties
    ↓
3. Presidential executive orders
    ↓
4. Federal agency rules and regulations
    ↓
5. Federal agency adjudication decisions
    ↓
6. State constitutions
    ↓
7. State statutes
    ↓
8. Gubernatorial executive orders
    ↓
9. State agency decisions
    ↓
10. Local ordinances
    ↓
11. Common law rulings

FIGURE 1.2.1   Hierarchy of Sources of Law in the United States

agency's jurisdiction. Federal agency rules and regulations have the force of law, and they often fill in the details of federal statutes.

All of these sources of law are replicated at the state level, and many states give local governments some limited law making powers as well. Local laws are often called **ordinances**. In general, the U.S. Constitution's **Supremacy Clause** makes the federal sources of law superior to the state sources of law, but state supreme courts generally have the last word on issues of pure state law where there is no federal constitutional question. For example, when in *Goodridge v. Department of Public Health* (2003) the Massachusetts Supreme Judicial Court interpreted its state constitution to require that the state allow same-sex marriages, the state supreme court was the last word on this issue, which was purely a matter of state law. Or when many states interpreted their state constitutions to require that the state legislature equalize funding among public school districts in the state, there was no federal issue presented and the state supreme courts were the last stop for these cases. States were able to do this because the U.S. Supreme Court previously ruled that there is no federal right to an education in *San Antonio Independent School District v. Rodriguez* (1973).

If there is no specific source of law in a particular case, judges many nevertheless make a decision in the name of justice. This last type of judicial decision is often referred to as **common law judicial rulings**. These judicial decisions are not based on a specific written source of law but nevertheless have the force of law themselves. For example, in the late 1800s, there were no statutes or agency administrative regulations covering most consumer products. Despite being unable to cite a specific source of law, judges made a variety of common law rulings that said that consumer products must be safe for their intended purposes. Thus, judges in the United States can and do interpret all of these sources of law in the hierarchy, and, unlike their colleagues in the civil law family of legal systems, they can make a decision even when no specific source of law is directly on point for the case at hand.

Legal Reasoning and Legal Analysis

The key difference between decision making in the courts and in other political institutions in the United States is the fact that judges must rely on legal analysis and legal reasoning in their decision-making process in addition to any political or ideological influences.[37] Courts are like other institutions of government because they make political and public-policy-based decisions. However, courts are different from other governmental actors because they are separate from the other institutions of government and because courts, or at least the federal courts, are seen as outside the mainstream of pure politics.[38] As Herman Pritchett, one of the fathers of the study of judicial politics, noted, "Political scientists who have done so much to put the 'political' in 'political jurisprudence' need to emphasize that it is still 'jurisprudence.' It is judging in a political context, but it is still judging; and judging is something different from legislating or administering."[39]

Legal reasoning involves viewing disputes through a neutral, analytical, and unemotional lens. Although the courts are clearly political institutions in our society, judges' use of legal reasoning and legal analysis mean that the courts are very different decision makers from the other institutions of government. Justice Anthony M. Kennedy, for instance, has noted that the Supreme Court was "set apart from other branches of government because it speaks a different language from the political branches."[40]

Thinking Like a Lawyer

Although judges do think and act politically, they must also think like lawyers instead of just thinking like politicians. Politicians do not always need to explain their decisions, but judges must always justify their rulings in terms of the rule of law and legal reasoning. In common law countries, all of a judge's rulings must be stated in such a way that they appear to be based on rules, principles, and doctrines external to the judge.[41] Or in other words, legal reasoning justifications for judicial decisions are necessary in our society, even if different judges would have different opinions in any given case due to a variety of political considerations. The notion that judges are constrained in their decision making by legal reasoning makes judges very different from politicians as decision makers.

Formality is very important in the law and legal reasoning. The courts must follow formal procedures, and they must apply formal rules to the facts before them. Their decisions are also delivered in a very formal fashion.[42] It is the job of lawyers and judges to understand the formal law and its language. The rules of the law focus more on form and authority rather than on morality and social context.[43] Thus, legal reasoning and legal analysis are quite rule oriented. As Frederick Schauer, a legal scholar, noted, "Reasoning with *rules* is perhaps the most common image of what lawyers and judges do."[44]

In addition to the careful use of language and a very specific analytical approach to problem solving, legal reasoning also requires the use of a certain process or procedure. That is, *how* decisions are made is often as important as *what* decisions are made. Legal analysis also includes a great deal of reasoning by analogy. And because American legal reasoning takes place in a common law legal system, the legal rules are often discovered by analyzing the precedents of appropriate appellate courts. Since judges are lawyers first, it is no accident that judges learn to "think like lawyers" in law school.[45] In addition, they must also learn to "think like judges," which means learning to act as a neutral arbiter between lawyers who are advocating for the interests of their clients. Therefore, legal reasoning involves careful use of language in a rule- and process-oriented analytical framework. (Chapter 4 covers law school and the legal profession in more detail.)

Decision Making According to the Law

American courts are independent decision makers. In part, this means that other political actors cannot dictate the legal rulings of judges. Justice Stephen G. Breyer, among others, has argued that judicial independence has its foundation in decision making according to the law, meaning that judges must follow specific sources of law and legal procedures when they make their decisions.[46] As mentioned earlier in the chapter, one key aspect of legal reasoning is the reliance on precedent. So although our federal courts are extremely independent and thus free from almost all forms of political control, they still must use legal analysis and the precedents of higher courts. In other words, judges are really only constrained in their decision making by legal reasoning and legal analysis.

The more Americans learn about the unique form of legal reasoning used by the courts, the more public support for the judiciary increases. One study argues that the general public increases their support for the courts when the judges anchor their decisions in legal values and symbols rather than in political ones.[47] Knowledge of how the courts make their decisions produces an understanding of the distinctive role of the judiciary in the American political system, reinforcing the view that courts are different. This study concludes, "[Courts] are different, and they are special, and they are therefore worthy of esteem."[48]

Types of Court Cases

Now that we have established a broad understanding of the roots of our judicial system, its position within the larger political landscape, and how our judges make decisions, let us take a look at the types of disputes that our courts typically handle. These disputes can be divided into several categories: criminal cases, civil cases, constitutional cases, and administrative law cases.

A **crime** is a wrong against society. In our country, the courts are the only institution with the power to punish criminals. These punishments can include, among other things, fines paid to the government, a prison sentence, or even death in certain cases. In a criminal court case, the **prosecutor** is the lawyer who represents the interests of society and argues against the defendant, who is represented by his or her own lawyer. The **criminal defendant** is the individual accused of the crime. The prosecutor must prove the defendant's guilt beyond a reasonable doubt. The way criminal cases are named—for example, *People v. Defendant, State v. Defendant, Commonwealth v. Defendant, United States v. Defendant*—indicate that the defendant is accused of breaking society's legal rules. The vast majority of crimes in the United States are based on state law, but there are also a smaller number of crimes that fall under laws enacted by the U.S. Congress. Both state and federal statutes spell out the specifics of a crime in our society and provide a range of possible punishments, but only judges can actually impose a criminal sentence on a particular defendant. The only exception is that the death penalty must be imposed by a jury. Under most circumstances, the prosecutor cannot appeal a trial court's finding that the defendant is not guilty. (For more about the criminal process in the United States, see Chapter 5.)

Civil cases in the United States involve wrongs between individuals broadly defined. The **plaintiff** is the one who files the civil lawsuit, while the **defendant** must defend it. Thus, a civil case could be *Smith v. Smith* (perhaps a divorce case), *Smith v. Jones* (perhaps a real property dispute), *Smith v. the U.S. Postal Service* (perhaps for a car accident with a postal truck), or *Smith v. Multinational Corporation* (perhaps a contract dispute or even an employment lawsuit). The case could also be *Netscape v. Microsoft* (perhaps an anti-trust case or a patent dispute). Some of these civil cases, such as divorces or probating a will, require a judge's signature in order to finalize the case. For other civil suits, the courts are available to help settle the dispute when alternatives fail. Courts also provide a neutral judge trained in the law who can help find the most just remedy to the dispute. Generally the plaintiff must prove a civil case by a preponderance of the evidence or perhaps by a higher standard known as clear and convincing evidence. If one were to use the scales of justice as a metaphor, a preponderance of evidence would tip the scales just a little in one direction, while clear and convincing evidence would tip the scales further. However, both burdens of proof used in civil cases are much less difficult to meet than the standard of guilt beyond a reasonable doubt, which prosecutors must prove in a criminal case. (See Chapter 6 for more on civil lawsuits.)

Administrative law cases require the courts to review the decisions made by governmental bureaucratic agencies to make sure that these decisions follow the proper processes and procedures. The interactions between courts and bureaucratic agencies in the executive branch of government will be discussed in more detail in Chapter 12. **Constitutional** interpretation are those in which the courts interpret the U.S. Constitution or the various state constitutions. The United States does not have separate courts for constitutional cases, as do the French and the Germans; rather, constitutional issues can arise in criminal, civil, and administrative law disputes handled by the regular courts in the United States.

Purposes of Courts in the United States

The prior discussion of the various types of cases hinted at some of the purposes of the courts in our nation. American courts can resolve disputes among individuals or groups, modify behavior, protect the rights of individuals, and make public policy. Courts can punish crimes. They can also serve as umpires in the disputes between Congress and the president, or between the federal government and the states. In general, courts resolve disputes in our society through their interpretations of multiple sources of law. Donald Kommers, a judicial politics scholar, nicely summed up the roles that courts play in the United States by noting, "From the nation's founding until today, courts have been a mainstay of American democracy. They settle legal conflicts between private parties, protect the legal rights of citizens generally, and supervise the administration of ordinary law."[49] Courts therefore serve a variety of purposes in our nation.

Courts as Policy Makers

One clear function of the courts in the United States is to make public policy, which renders them different from courts in many societies. This is often done through the courts' use of their power of judicial review. **Judicial review** is the power of the courts to determine the constitutionality of the actions of other political actors such as Congress, the president, the bureaucracy, or the states. By interpreting the U.S. Constitution and other sources of law, courts in the United States make many public policies that would be made legislatively or bureaucratically in other nations. For example, using its power of judicial review, the U.S. Supreme Court has handed down a variety of decisions that result in a specific public policy outcome, such as the right of women to choose to have an abortion (*Roe v. Wade*, 1973) or the principle that legislative districts must be almost precisely equal in population (*Baker v. Carr*, 1962). The U.S. Supreme Court has declared that there is an individual right to privacy that the government cannot infringe upon (*Griswold v. Connecticut*, 1965) and decreed that burning the American flag as a form of political protest cannot be criminalized (*Texas v. Johnson*, 1989). The U.S. Supreme Court outlawed discrimination by race in our public schools through its power of judicial review (*Brown v. Board of Education*, 1954), while state supreme courts in Massachusetts and Iowa, among others, have interpreted their state constitutions to require that same-sex marriages be allowed. In addition to making public policy, some also argue that the courts should protect the interests of political minorities that cannot or will not be protected in the more majoritarian institutions of government such as the legislative and executive branches.

In some ways this power of judicial review is uniquely American, although courts in other societies are beginning to exercise this great power with increasing frequency.[50] Technically courts in the United Kingdom and New Zealand do not have the power of judicial review at all,[51] and courts in Canada only formally received this power with the enactment of the Charter of Rights and Freedoms in 1982. However, since that date the Canadian courts have been quite activist in using their power of judicial review.[52] The noticeable difference between judicial review in Canada and the United States is that legislative bodies in Canada can vote to maintain a statute in effect even if the courts have declared it to be unconstitutional.[53] The Canadians refer to this as the "notwithstanding" power of the provinces. The German Constitutional Court also utilizes a form of judicial review,[54] as do constitutional courts in various other societies.[55] Almost no courts elsewhere in the world have used their power of judicial review and its resulting policy-making ability to the extent that they are utilized in the United States. While American judges certainly make public policy to a greater degree than most of their international colleagues, they must nevertheless do so through the lens of legal reasoning and legal analysis. When considering the power of judicial review, most Americans think only of the decisions of the U.S. Supreme Court. But the fact is that all regular courts in the United States can exercise the power of judicial review. For example, after voters in California outlawed same-sex marriage in Proposition 8, a federal trial court in California declared that action to be unconstitutional. For complex procedural reasons, the U.S. Supreme Court allowed the trial court's decision to become law in California. Same-sex marriages resumed in that state in 2013.

Dispute Resolution and Behavior Modification

Trial court decisions may illustrate other purposes of the courts. All changes in legal status must have a judge's order for the change to be implemented. For example, one cannot get a divorce without a judge's decree, nor can one change the status of a child's legal custody or an individual change his or her legal name without a court order. Changes in property ownership after a person's death or changes in real property boundaries also require a judge's order. Most other civil disputes do not require a judge to settle the dispute, although the courts are available when alternative dispute resolution mechanisms do not resolve the conflict. Courts also serve as institutions that encourage behavior modification for the parties involved and/or for the broader American public. Punitive damages awarded in civil cases often have the effect of modifying the behavior of similar parties in the future.

Civil cases serve a variety of other purposes as well. For example, no capitalist society can function without clear and consistent rules of contract law. Courts must decide which contracts are enforceable and what legal remedies are available when contract bargains are breached. Courts also must protect the public from potential bargains that violate public policy and are thus considered unenforceable.[56] In addition, inventors need predictable patent and other intellectual property rules. Buyers and sellers of real estate need predictable real property laws. Civil cases can also be key tools for modernizing rules and procedures within bureaucratic agencies such as local police forces or municipal agencies that install and maintain playground equipment in local parks.[57] Occasionally when Congress and the state legislatures refuse to enact legislation on a specific topic because their members see it as being politically unpopular, the problem gets passed on to the courts, where judges find ways to solve the issue on a case-by-case basis.[58] For example, when anti-smoking activists could not convince Congress to pass tough anti-tobacco laws, they turned instead to a series of civil lawsuits to get rulings that they felt would better protect public health.[59]

The outcome of a particular civil case is important to the parties to the lawsuit, but the collective decisions in these civil cases can create important public policy results and can even help inform legislators what changes need to be made to various laws. In other words, "the accumulation of similar individual decisions defines policy just as much as one major decision [does]."[60] Civil cases help settle individual disputes, but, taken together, rulings in civil cases are another way that American courts make important public policy decisions.

Judges as Umpires Among Institutions

Another purpose of the courts is to serve as a referee between the other institutions of government, thus preventing any single political actor from gaining too much power in our nation. Some constitutionally based court decisions fall into this category. This judicial role of umpire is part of the separation of powers theory in the United States.[61] The concept of **separation of powers** means that governmental power is divided into distinct and separate functions, known as the executive, legislative, and judicial branches of government. Under the traditional notion of separation of powers, each branch of government has its own particular job to do. Our system of government is further complicated by the fact that we are a federal system, with distinct state and federal governments. **Federalism** is the division of power between the national government and the regional governments (in the United States, these are states), with the national government being supreme. In short, the United States has both a federal court system and fifty-one state court systems sharing the same geographical space, and it has separation of powers at both the federal and state levels. (I say that there are fifty-one state court systems because the local courts in the District of Columbia function just like a state court system for these purposes.)

One of the major duties of the judiciary is to help settle disputes between the legislative and executive branches of the federal government and between different levels of government, including disputes between the federal government and the states.[62] Because courts use legal reasoning in their decision-making process, judges carry out a special function in our democracy, often acting as a counterbalance to other governmental actors.[63] In order to serve as an umpire in these potential conflicts between other institutions of government, the courts must remain free from the control of any political actors. This is known as **judicial independence**, meaning that courts must be able to make their decisions without interference by the other branches and without fear that other political actors will directly retaliate against the judges because of their legal decisions. A competing value is **judicial accountability**, meaning that the courts and judges should be accountable to the voters. In general, our federal court system promotes the value of judicial independence, while most state court judicial selection systems promote the principle of judicial accountability. More details about the concepts of judicial independence and judicial accountability can be found in the discussion of judicial selection methods in Chapter 3.

The role of the courts in these institutional disputes can sometimes get quite messy, even though the courts are an independent third branch of government charged in part with serving as the umpire in these inter-institutional conflicts. The day-to-day workings of the separation of powers concept in the United States are not simplistic or clear-cut.[64] Instead of a simple and straightforward separation of powers, we in the United States have "separated institutions sharing powers."[65] In addition, federalism issues in our nation can become extremely complex.[66] We even fought the bloody Civil War in part over competing notions of federalism. Thus, the courts often come into conflict with other political actors in their role as umpire of separation of powers and federalism cases.

Some would argue, however, that these almost constant institutional conflicts are beneficial for our society in the long run. Robert Katzmann, a former professor who is now a federal judge on the U.S. Court of Appeals for the Second Circuit, spent a great deal of his academic career examining the interactions between the courts and the other branches. Katzmann argues, "Governance in the United States is a process of interaction among institutions—legislative, executive, and judicial—with separate and sometimes clashing structures, purposes, and interests. The Founders envisioned that constructive tension among those institutions would not only preserve liberty but would also promote the public good."[67]

Further Thoughts on the Power of Judicial Review

As mentioned earlier in the chapter, judicial review means the power of the courts to determine the constitutionality of the actions of other political actors, including Congress, the president, the federal bureaucracy, and the states. In interpreting the Constitution, the courts also serve as a check on the power of other political actors. In addition to being part of the common law family of legal systems, all the regular American courts have the tool of judicial review at their disposal, thus making our courts very powerful indeed. As Tocqueville noted, "Restricted within its limits, the power granted to American courts to pronounce on the constitutionality of laws is yet one of the most powerful barriers ever erected against the tyranny of political assemblies."[68]

Although the U.S. Constitution is silent on which body should interpret its provisions, in *Marbury v. Madison* (1803) the Supreme Court of the United States decided that it should be the primary interpreter of the Constitution, adopting the power of judicial review. The Court's decision in *Marbury* is consistent with Alexander Hamilton's views as he stated them in Federalist No. 78. The **Federalist Papers** were written by Alexander Hamilton, James Madison, and John Jay to persuade the states to ratify the U.S. Constitution. Federalist No. 78 argues that the new federal courts would have the power of judicial review. In arguing for the ratification of the new Constitution, Hamilton wrote, "No legislative act, therefore, contrary to the Constitution can be valid. ... The interpretation of the laws is the proper and peculiar province of the courts. A constitution is, in fact, and must be regarded by the judges as a fundamental law." Certainly almost all Americans agree today that all of the regular courts in the country have the power to determine the constitutionality of the actions of other political actors, including Congress, the president, the bureaucracy, and the states.

Originalism or a Living Constitution

However, scholars and judges often disagree about how the Constitution should be interpreted when courts exercise their power of judicial review. One clear debate is between those who advocate for an originalist approach to constitutional interpretation and those who see the Constitution as a living document whose interpretation must change as the society evolves. A third group is the pragmatists, who utilize more of a case-by-case approach to constitutional interpretation.

Originalism is the belief that the Constitution should be interpreted as the Framers intended. It is somewhat similar to an approach that says that the words of the Constitution should be read literally. These approaches are often collectively called *strict constructionism* or *literalism.*[69] That is, the meaning of the Constitution is fixed by the intent of the Framers.[70] Originalists therefore see the Constitution as a binding contract whose principles can be changed only by constitutional amendment, not through judicial interpretation. One of the founders of the current originalism movement was Edwin Meese III, the U.S. attorney general during the Reagan Administration. In advocating an originalist or literalist interpretation of the Constitution, Attorney General Meese stated, "We know that those who framed the Constitution chose their words carefully. They debated at great length the minutest points. The language they chose meant something."[71] The core of originalism is the belief that fidelity to the original understanding of the Constitution should constrain contemporary judges. Originalists claim that judges need neutral, objective criteria in order to make legitimate decisions that the people will respect, and that the Framers' intent provides those neutral criteria. As Meese explained, "The great genius of the constitutional blueprint is found in its creation and respect for spheres of authority and the limits it places on governmental power."[72] For originalists, the main way to promote the rule of law is to prevent judges from reading into the Constitution their own personal political philosophies. As Steven Calabresi, the co-founder of the Federalist Society (a group of conservative judges, law professors, law students, and others who promote originalism), wrote, "There is no liberal or conservative meaning of the text of the Constitution; there is only a right meaning and a wrong meaning."[73] Originalism, according to its advocates, ensures that judges choose the right meaning of the Constitution.

Justice Antonin Scalia has often been considered one of the leading proponents of originalism, even though he claims his approach is more nuanced than that of most originalists and he openly rejects the literalist label. Justice Scalia has written, "Twenty years ago, when I joined the Supreme Court, I was the only originalist among its members."[74] Today, most commentators would count at least four originalists on the Court. Justice Scalia has often said that the Constitution is dead—that is, its meaning cannot change over time.[75] In arguing for originalism, Justice Scalia wrote, "Our manner of interpreting the Constitution is to begin with the text, and to give that text the meaning that it bore when it was adopted by the people."[76] Thus, in the eyes of Justice Scalia and other originalists, the original intent of the Framers is almost sacred. Justice Scalia argues that, unless courts interpret the

Constitution according to the intent of the Framers, unelected federal judges will improperly impose their own personal policy preferences on our society.[77] And this is exactly what has happened, according to Justice Scalia. He notes, "So it is literally true, and I don't think this is an exaggeration, that the Court has essentially liberated itself from the text of the Constitution, from the text, and even from the traditions of the American people."[78] For originalists, the cure for this constitutional ill is originalism. As Justice Scalia has stated, "Originalism seems to me more compatible with the nature and purpose of a Constitution in a democratic system."[79] In short, originalists want to restrain the power and influence of federal judges, who are appointed for life, and prevent them from imposing their own values and ideologies on the American public through judicial fiat, or decree.

Justices William J. Brennan and Thurgood Marshall were among the chief proponents of a competing approach, often known as the **living Constitution theory**, which holds that the Constitution is a living and changing document that judges should interpret and reinterpret with a modern eye. That is, constitutional interpretation must evolve as the society evolves. They believed that current judges cannot know the intent of the Framers, in part, because a collective group cannot have a single intent. They also argued that judges should use their expertise to produce justice in a particular case, regardless of how the Constitution had been interpreted in the past. Justice Brennan was a strong critic of originalism, and of it he said:

> In truth it is little more than arrogance cloaked as humility. It is arrogant to pretend that from our vantage we can gauge accurately the intent of the Framers on application of principle to specific, contemporary questions. [...] For the genius of the Constitution rests not in any static meaning it might have had in a world that is dead and gone, but in the adaptability of its great principles to cope with current problems and current needs. What the constitutional fundamentals meant to the wisdom of other times cannot be their measure to the vision of our time.[80]

Justice Marshall took a similar approach. Being the first African American to serve on the Supreme Court, he was especially sensitive to how the Framers treated people of color. He did not approve of the way the original Constitution handled the issues of slavery and constitutional rights for people of African descent. In a 1987 speech, Justice Marshall declared, "I do not believe that the meaning of the Constitution was forever 'fixed' at the Philadelphia Convention. Nor do I find the wisdom, foresight, and sense of justice exhibited by the framers particularly profound."[81] Justices Brennan and Marshall believed that the Constitution should be interpreted in such a way as to protect the most vulnerable in our society.

One of the contemporary examples of the living Constitution concept is when the Supreme Court uses the term "evolving standards of decency" to interpret the Eighth Amendment's ban on cruel and unusual punishments. The phrase was first used in *Trop v. Dulles* (1958), where the Court ruled that it was unconstitutional for the government to revoke the citizenship of a U.S. citizen as a punishment for a crime. In that case, the majority opinion stated that "the words of the [Eighth] Amendment are not precise, and that their scope is not static. The Amendment must draw its meaning from the evolving standards of decency that mark the progress of a maturing society."[82] The Court again used the phrase "evolving standards of decency" in *Atkins v. Virginia* (2002), where it declared that the mentally disabled cannot be executed under the Eighth Amendment.[83] This phrase was also used in *Roper v. Simmons* (2005), where the Supreme Court declared it unconstitutional to execute defendants who were juveniles when they committed the crime.[84] An even stronger statement of the living Constitution doctrine came in Justice John Paul Stevens's concurrence in *Roper*. He wrote:

> Perhaps even more important than our specific holding today is our reaffirmation of the basic principle that informs the Court's interpretation of the *Eighth Amendment*. If the meaning of that Amendment had been frozen when it was originally drafted, it would impose no impediment to the execution of 7-year-old children today. The evolving standards of decency that have driven our construction of this critically important part of the Bill of Rights foreclose any such reading of the Amendment. In the best tradition of the common law, the pace of that evolution is a matter for continuing debate; but that our understanding of the Constitution does change from time to time has been settled since John Marshall breathed life into its text. If great lawyers of his day—Alexander Hamilton, for example—were sitting with us today, I would expect them to join Justice Kennedy's opinion for the Court.[85]

In a similar fashion to the Living Constitutionalists, but promoting a third approach, Justice Stephen Breyer argues that judges should be pragmatic in their interpretations of the Constitution: "The Court should reject approaches to interpreting the Constitution that consider the document's scope and application as fixed at the moment of framing. Rather, the Court should regard the Constitution as containing unwavering values that must be applied flexibly to ever-changing circumstances."[86] Thus, Justice Breyer advocates a pragmatic judicial approach that "hesitates to rely on any single theory or grand view of law, of interpretation, or of the Constitution."[87] Judge Richard Posner of the U.S. Court of Appeals for the Seventh Circuit is a prolific writer and commentator on the law, as well as being a judge. Although he is much more conservative than Justice Breyer, Judge Posner also advocates a pragmatic approach to legal questions, stating, "The word that best describes the average American judge at all levels of our judicial hierarchies and yields the greatest insight into his behavior is 'pragmatist.'"[88] Scholars who promote a more pragmatic reading of the Constitution are usually critical of originalism. They often note that the literal wording of the Constitution or the intent of the Framers provides very little guidance about how to decide particular cases.[89] Many contemporary judges are pragmatists because they routinely consider policy, the principles behind the law, and the law's consequences in their decisions.[90]

In this debate, we should be cautious about several things. First, among the justices who claim that they are properly interpreting the intent of the Framers are many who strongly disagree with one another about what that intent might be. For example, in *District of Columbia v. Heller* (2008), both the majority opinion and the dissent forcefully claimed that they were properly interpreting the intent of the Framers in writing the Second Amendment. This case involved the District of Columbia's very tough gun control law, which the majority declared unconstitutional because it violated an individual's right to bear arms. The dissenting justices would have upheld the gun control law because they believed the Framers intended the Second Amendment to protect only the state's collective right to have an armed militia (known today as a national guard).

Second, many judges who use the rhetoric of originalism are in fact acting and voting in the manner of a judicial activist, a concept discussed in more detail below.[91] This often occurs when judges use the language of original intent to declare a statute or a government official's action unconstitutional. Third, ideological considerations may often outweigh a justice's preferred philosophy of decision making. In fact, several studies[92] have found that for many justices, "commitment to an ideological direction was far stronger than commitment to a mode of constitutional interpretation."[93] Thus, we must look beyond the words of judges to see how they are actually using their power of judicial review.

Judicial Activism Versus Judicial Restraint

Although there is widespread agreement that American courts now have the power of judicial review, there is far less agreement on how judges should use this immense power. There are two main competing judicial philosophies that judges use to help guide them in their use of their power of judicial review—judicial activism and judicial restraint. There is a great deal of debate in the academic community on the precise definitions of these philosophies. Although the dispute between originalism and the concept of a living Constitution forms part of the basis for these competing judicial philosophies, the debate between judicial activists and judicial restraintists is much broader than that more narrow interpretive approach.

Judicial activism is especially hard to define analytically because many people attach the label to any court decisions with which they disagree.[94] Thus, *judicial activism* can be a loaded term that has multiple meanings and politicized connotations, especially as used by politicians.[95] This book, however, will use the terms *judicial activism* and *judicial restraint* in a more analytical and academic sense, which can and often does differ from the way the terms may be used in broader political debates. While some would argue that the definition of judicial activism should include situations where the Supreme Court and other appellate judges overturn existing precedent, I think we should instead define these terms according to the relationship between the courts and other actors. Therefore, I think judicial activism and restraint should be defined not according to what judges say, but in terms of what they actually do.

There are three parts to our definition of **judicial activism**. First, activist judges tend to interpret the U.S. Constitution as a living and changing document that needs to be reinterpreted as society evolves. While they might use the language of originalism, their actions in updating the meaning of the Constitution speak louder than their rhetoric. Second, judicial activists see making public policy as a natural part of the purpose of the courts in our nation. Third, activist judges tend to be quite willing to declare the actions of other political actors to be unconstitutional. Thus, judicial activism typically occurs when judges make decisions that promote justice in alignment with a changing society, and when a court declares something to be unconstitutional.

Although activists can be either liberal or conservative, most commentators today first think of liberal judicial activism. Examples of famous liberal activist decisions include *Brown v. Board of Education* (1954), which declared racial segregation in public schools to be unconstitutional; *Miranda v. Arizona* (1966), which requires police to read criminal defendants their rights at the point of arrest; *Roe v. Wade* (1973), which declared unconstitutional fifty state abortion laws; and *Texas v. Johnson* (1989), which declared unconstitutional laws prohibiting the burning of the American flag as a form of political protest.

Judicial restraint, on the other hand, uses the opposite approach. Restraintists are uncomfortable with judges' immense power of judicial review. They want to restrict the circumstances under which judges may actually use this power. Thus, restraintists tend to believe that the Constitution should be interpreted only as the Framers intended. Second, judicial restraintists believe that the courts should not be policy makers but instead should make only purely legal decisions, much like the courts in the United Kingdom. Finally, restraintists do not often exercise their power of judicial review, instead deferring to the decisions of the elected branches of government. Therefore, judicial restraint occurs whenever a court upholds the constitutionality of the actions of other governmental actors. Some recent examples of judicial restraint are *Bowers v. Hardwick* (1986), where the Supreme Court refused to declare Georgia's anti-sodomy law to be unconstitutional, and *Gonzales v. Carhart* (2007), where the Supreme Court upheld a federal law banning the use of a late-term abortion technique known by its opponents as partial-birth abortion. Another example of judicial restraint was *National Federation of Independent Business v. Sebelius* (2012), where the Supreme Court upheld as constitutional most of President Obama's Affordable Care Act (see Chapter 10 for more details about this case).

As mentioned earlier, the differences between judicial activism and judicial restraint do not break along strictly ideological lines. From the late 1800s until 1936, the Supreme Court was dominated by conservative judicial activists, who prevented most regulation of economic activities in the United States by reading an unyielding right to contract into the Fourteenth Amendment.[96] The Warren Court of the 1950s and 1960s was clearly dominated by liberal judicial activists, who saw the role of the Supreme Court as protecting the most vulnerable political minorities in our society.[97] Today, the Supreme Court hands down both liberal activist decisions and conservative activist ones, depending on the issue.[98] As one influential scholar has argued, the Supreme Court under Chief Justice William Rehnquist in the 1990s and early 2000s was the most activist Court in history because it issued many liberal activist decisions and many conservative activist decisions.[99]

Today, even some conservatives—specifically those who want courts to have a smaller role in deciding controversial national issues—are upset by the recent trend of conservative judicial activism on the Supreme Court.[100] Many of Justice Scalia's critics, for example, believe that his voting behavior in reality reflects conservative activism despite his rhetoric in favor of originalism.[101] The Tea Party movement in the United States seems to advocate for an extreme version of judicial restraint. As scholars Theda Skocpol and Vanessa Williamson have written, "A tour of Tea Party websites around the country quickly reveals widespread determination to restore twenty-first century U.S. government to the Constitutional principles articulated by the eighteenth-century Founding Fathers."[102] These scholars continue, "A persistent refrain in Tea Party circles is the scorn for politicians who fail to show suitable reverence for, and detailed mastery of, America's founding documents."[103] Examples of recent liberal activist decisions include *Lawrence v. Texas* (2003), which declared the Texas anti-sodomy statute unconstitutional and overturned the Court's previous decision in *Bowers,* and *Miller v. Alabama* (2012), which declared unconstitutional mandatory life sentences without parole for juvenile offenders. Some examples of recent conservative activist decisions include *Citizens United v. Federal Election Commission* (2010), which declared unconstitutional federal statutory limits on the amount of money corporations and unions could spend on political campaigns, and *District of Columbia v. Heller* (2008), which declared unconstitutional the gun control laws in D.C. because the majority decided that the Second Amendment provides for an individual right to own guns.

Governance as Dialogue

The concepts of judicial review, judicial activism, and judicial restraint all lead to the question of what the proper role of the Supreme Court in the American political system should be. The **Governance as Dialogue movement** argues that the Supreme Court is not the last word on interpreting the Constitution but instead is part of a continuing inter-institutional conversation. Therefore, the meaning of the Constitution is eventually determined by a continuing discussion among various political actors and institutions. As one research study concluded, "American political institutions by design are inextricably linked in a continuing dialogue."[104] Some scholars have argued that public policy making in this country is a "dynamic process" in which "issues recur."[105] Justice Ruth Bader Ginsburg has stated that constitutional interpretation often requires courts to enter into "a continuing dialogue with other branches of government, the States, or the private sector."[106] As Justice Robert H. Jackson argued more than fifty years ago, "No sound assessment of our Supreme Court can treat it as an isolated, self-sustaining, or self-sufficient institution. It is a unit of a complex, interdependent scheme of government from which it cannot be severed."[107] Thus, the Governance as Dialogue movement looks at how all the institutions of government interact and negotiate the meaning of the Constitution. As one member of Congress told me in an interview, "The relationship between Congress and the courts involves a continuous back and forth between us and the courts. In other words, it is a complex dialogue among equal branches always jockeying for power."[108]

Unlike the other political actors taking part in the continuing conversation or dialogue about the meaning of the Constitution, the courts bring a unique voice to the table because judges must justify their decisions using legal reasoning and legal analysis. Therefore, the Supreme Court should be part of this continuing inter-institutional dialogue about the meaning of the Constitution. This book is written very much in the spirit of the Governance as Dialogue approach.

Outline of the Remainder of the Book

The first chapter of this text has examined the functions and purposes of courts in American society, our common law roots, the sources of law our judges use, and the basics of legal analysis. It has also presented some basic vocabulary that is essential to an understanding of judicial politics. Chapter 2 is devoted to exploring the structure of American courts. The next section of the book, Chapters 3 and 4, will examine in more detail the role of lawyers and judges, who are crucial players in the judicial system, as well as both the state and federal judicial selection processes. Chapters 5 and 6 will look at the role of trial courts, first in criminal cases and then in civil cases. Chapters 7 and 8 will consider the policy-making role of appellate courts and how political scientists study judicial decision making on these courts.

The last half of the book will examine the interactions between courts and other political actors, beginning in Chapter 9 with the interactions between the courts and interest groups, the media, and the general public. Chapters 10, 11, and 12 look at the interactions between courts and legislatures, courts and presidents or governors, and courts and bureaucratic agencies. The final chapter examines the interactions between courts in the United States with courts abroad. The goal of the entire book is to give the reader a better understanding of judicial politics in the United States.

For Further Reading

Breyer, Stephen. 2010. *Making Our Democracy Work: A Judge's View.* New York: Alfred A. Knopf.

Carter, Lief H., and Thomas F. Burke. 2010. *Reason in Law.* 8th ed. New York: Longman.

Keck, Thomas. 2004. *The Most Activist Supreme Court in History: The Road to Modern Judicial Conservatism.* Chicago: University of Chicago Press.

Lindquist, Stefanie A., and Frank B. Cross. 2009. *Measuring Judicial Activism.* New York: Oxford University Press.

Scalia, Antonin. 1997. *A Matter of Interpretation: Federal Courts and the Law.* Princeton, NJ: Princeton University Press.

Schauer, Frederick. 2009. *Thinking Like a Lawyer: A New Introduction to Legal Reasoning.* Cambridge, MA: Harvard University Press.

Silverstein, Gordon. 2009. *Law's Allure: How Law Shapes, Constrains, Saves, and Kills Politics.* New York: Cambridge University Press.

Tate, C. Neal, and Torbjorn Vallinder, eds. 1995. *The Global Expansion of Judicial Power.* New York: New York University Press.

Vandevelde, Kenneth J. 2010. *Thinking Like a Lawyer: An Introduction to Legal Reasoning.* 2nd ed. Boulder, CO: Westview.

Van Geel, T. R. 2009. *Understanding Supreme Court Opinions.* 6th ed. New York: Pearson Longman.

Notes

1. See, e.g., C. Neal Tate and Torbjorn Vallinder, eds., *The Global Expansion of Judicial Power* (New York: New York University Press, 1995).

2. Robert A. Kagan, "American Courts and the Policy Dialogue: The Role of Adversarial Legalism," in Mark C. Miller and Jeb Barnes, eds., *Making Policy, Making Law: An Interbranch Perspective* (Washington, DC: Georgetown University Press, 2004), 24.

3. Martin Shapiro and Alec Stone, "The New Constitutional Politics of Europe," *Comparative Political Studies* 26 (1994): 397–420.

4. Martin Shapiro, "The United States," in C. Neal Tate and Torbjorn Vallinder, eds., *The Global Expansion of Judicial Power* (New York: New York University Press, 1995), 43.

5. Gillian K. Hadfield and Barry R. Weingast, "Law Without the State: Legal Attributes and the Coordination of Decentralized Collective Punishment," *Journal of Law and Courts* 1 (2013): 3–34.

6. Sheryl L. Grna, Jane C. Ollenburger, and Mark Nicholas, *The Social Context of Law*, 2nd ed. (Upper Saddle River, NJ: Prentice Hall, 2002), 14.

7. Elizabeth Mertz, *The Language of Law School: Learning to Think like a Lawyer* (New York: Oxford University Press, 2007), 3.

8. Lief H. Carter and Thomas F. Burke, *Reason in Law*, 8th ed. (New York: Longman, 2010), 8.

9. David B. Brinkerhoff, Lynn K. White, and Suzanne Trager Ortega, *Essentials of Sociology*, 3rd ed. (Minneapolis: West Publishing, 1995), 39.

10. Sanford Levinson, "Foreword," in Lief H. Carter and Thomas F. Burke, eds., *Reason in Law*, 8th ed. (New York: Longman, 2010), viii.

11. Harold D. Lasswell, *Politics: Who Gets What, When, How* (Ann Arbor: University of Michigan Press, 1936).

12. David Easton, *The Political System: An Inquiry into the State of Political Science* (New York: Knopf, 1953), 126.

13. Keith E. Whittington, R. Daniel Kelemen, and Gregory A. Caldeira, "The Study of Law and Politics," in Keith E. Whittington, R. Daniel Kelemen, and Gregory A. Caldeira, eds., *The Oxford Handbook of Law and Politics* (New York: Oxford University Press, 2008), 3.

14. Ibid., 9.

15. Walter F. Murphy, C. Herman Pritchett, Lee Epstein, and Jack Knight, *Courts, Judges, and Politics: An Introduction to the Judicial Process*, 6th ed. (New York: McGraw-Hill, 2005), 3.

16. Herbert Jacob, "Introduction," in Herbert Jacob, Erhard Blankenburg, Herbert M. Kritzer, Doris Marie Provine, and Joseph Sanders, eds., *Courts, Law, and Politics in a Comparative Perspective* (New Haven: Yale University Press, 1996), 1.

17. Donald P. Kommers, "American Courts and Democracy: A Comparative Perspective," in Kermit L. Hall and Kevin T. McGuire, eds., *The Judicial Branch* (New York: Oxford University Press, 2005), 200–201.

18. Twenty-five of the fifty-two signers of the Declaration of Independence were lawyers, as were thirty-one of the fifty-five members of the Continental Congress. Esther Lucile Brown, *Lawyers, Law Schools, and the Public Service* (New York: Russell Sage Foundation, 1948), 17.

19. Mark C. Miller, *The High Priests of American Politics: The Role of Lawyers in American Political Institutions* (Knoxville: University of Tennessee Press, 1995).

20. Sandra Day O'Connor, "Foreword," in Norman Gross, ed., *America's Lawyer-Presidents: From Law Office to Oval Office* (Evanston, IL: Northwestern University Press, 2004), ix.

21. Norman Gross, "Introduction," in Norman Gross, ed., *America's Lawyer-Presidents: From Law Office to Oval Office* (Evanston, IL: Northwestern University Press, 2004), xv.

22. See Robert A. Kagan, *Adversarial Legalism: The American Way of Law* (Cambridge, MA: Harvard University Press, 2001).

23. Alexis de Tocqueville, *Democracy in America*, trans. George Lawrence (New York: Harper and Row, 1966), 99.

24. Frederick Schauer, *Thinking Like a Lawyer: A New Introduction to Legal Reasoning* (Cambridge, MA: Harvard University Press, 2009), 103–106.

25. H. Patrick Glenn, *Legal Traditions of the World* (New York: Oxford University Press, 2000).

26. Tom Ginsburg, *Judicial Review in New Democracies: Constitutional Courts in Asian Cases* (Cambridge: Cambridge University Press, 2003).

27. Murphy et al., *Courts, Judges, and Politics*, 7.

28. Schauer, *Thinking Like a Lawyer*, 107.

29. Murphy et al., *Courts, Judges, and Politics*, 5.

30. Ibid., 7.

31. See, e.g., James V. Calvi and Susan Coleman, *American Law and Legal Systems*, 7th ed. (Boston: Longman, 2012), 6–7.

32. Richard A. Posner, *How Judges Think* (Cambridge, MA: Harvard University Press, 2008), 232.

33. See, e.g., Laurence Tribe, "Clarence Thomas and 'Natural Law,'" *New York Times,* July 15, 1991.

34. Calvi and Coleman, *American Law and Legal Systems*, 7.

35. Graham G. Dodds, *Take Up Your Pen: Unilateral Presidential Directives in American Politics* (Philadelphia: University of Pennsylvania Press, 2013).

36. Lyn Ragsdale, *Presidential Politics* (Boston: Houghton Mifflin, 1993), 74–75.

37. Carter and Burke, *Reason in Law.*

38. Lawrence Baum, "The Future of the Judicial Branch: Courts and Democracy in the Twenty-First Century," in Kermit L. Hall and Kevin T. McGuire, eds., *The Judicial Branch* (New York: Oxford University Press, 2005), 517.

39. C. Herman Pritchett, "The Development of Judicial Research," in Joel Grossman and Joseph Tanenhaus, eds., *Frontiers of Judicial Research* (New York: Wiley, 1969), 42.

40. Quoted in Barbara A. Perry, *The Priestly Tribe: The Supreme Court's Image in the American Mind* (Westport, CT: Praeger, 1999), 48.

41. T. R. Van Geel, *Understanding Supreme Court Opinions*, 6th ed. (New York: Pearson Longman, 2009), 48.

42. William Haltom, *Reporting on the Courts: How the Mass Media Cover Judicial Actions* (Chicago: Nelson-Hall, 1998), 30.

43. Mertz, *The Language of Law School*, 4.

44. Schauer, *Thinking Like a Lawyer*, 13.

45. William M. Sullivan, Anne Colby, Judith Welch Wegner, Lloyd Bond, and Lee S. Shulman, *Educating Lawyers: Preparation for the Profession of Law* (San Francisco: Wiley, 2007).

46. Stephen G. Breyer, "Judicial Independence in the United States," *St. Louis University Law Review* 40 (1996): 989–996.

47. Gregory A. Caldeira and James L. Gibson, "The Etiology of Public Support for the Supreme Court," *American Journal of Political Science* 36 (1992): 635–664, at 659.

48. James L. Gibson and Gregory A. Caldeira, *Citizens, Courts, and Confirmations: Positivity Theory and the Judgments of the American People* (Princeton, NJ: Princeton University Press, 2009), 122.

49. Kommers, "American Courts and Democracy," 200–201.

50. Tate and Vallinder, eds., *The Global Expansion of Judicial Power*.

51. Herbert M. Kritzer, "Courts, Justice, and Politics in England," in Herbert Jacob, Erhard Blankenburg, Herbert M. Kritzer, Doris Marie Provine, and Joseph Sanders, eds., *Courts, Law, and Politics in a Comparative Perspective* (New Haven, CT: Yale University Press, 1996), 82.

52. Peter H. Russell and David M. O'Brien, eds., *Judicial Independence in the Age of Democracy: Critical Perspectives from Around the World* (Charlottesville: University Press of Virginia, 2001).

53. Stephen Breyer, *Making Democracy Work: A Judge's View* (New York: Alfred A. Knopf, 2010), 3.

54. Erhard Blankenburg, "Changes in Political Regimes and Continuity of the Rule of Law in Germany," in Herbert Jacob, Erhard Blankenburg, Herbert M. Kritzer, Doris Marie Provine, and Joseph Sanders, eds., *Courts, Law, and Politics in a Comparative Perspective* (New Haven: Yale University Press, 1996).

55. See Mark Tushnet, *Weak Courts, Strong Rights: Judicial Review and Social Welfare Rights in Comparative Constitutional Law* (Princeton, NJ: Princeton University Press, 2009).

56. Lawrence A. Cunningham, *Contracts in the Real World: Stories of Popular Contracts and Why They Matter* (New York: Cambridge University Press, 2012), 5.

57. See Charles R. Epp, *Making Rights Real: Activists, Bureaucrats, and the Creation of the Legalistic State* (Chicago: University of Chicago Press, 2009).

58. Jeb Barnes, *Dust-up: Asbestos Litigation and the Failure of Commonsense Policy Reform* (Washington, DC: Georgetown University Press, 2011), 12–13.

59. Martha A. Derthick, *Up in Smoke: From Legislation to Litigation in Tobacco Politics*, 2nd ed. (Washington, DC: CQ Press, 2005).

60. Lynn Mather, "The Fired Football Coach (Or, How Trial Courts Make Policy)," in Lee Epstein, ed., *Contemplating Courts* (Washington, DC: CQ Press, 1995).

61. Jeb Barnes, "Adversarial Legalism, the Rise of Judicial Policymaking, and the Separation-of-Powers Doctrine," in Mark C. Miller and Jeb Barnes, eds., *Making Policy, Making Law: An Interbranch Perspective* (Washington, DC: Georgetown University Press, 2004).

62. Koen Lenerts, "Constitutionalism and the Many Faces of Federalism," *American Journal of Comparative Law* 38 (1990): 205–264.

63. Baum, "The Future of the Judicial Branch," 517.

64. Barnes, "Adversarial Legalism."

65. Richard E. Neustadt, *Presidential Power: The Politics of Leadership from FDR to Carter* (New York: Wiley, 1980), 26.

66. Daniel Halberstam, "Comparative Federalism and the Role of the Judiciary," in Keith E. Whittington, R. Daniel Kelemen, and Gregory A. Caldeira, eds., *The Oxford Handbook of Law and Politics* (New York: Oxford University Press, 2008).

67. Robert A. Katzmann, *Courts and Congress* (Washington, DC: Brookings Institution Press, 1997), 1.

68. Tocqueville, *Democracy in America*, 103–104.

69. Antonin Scalia, *A Matter of Interpretation: Federal Courts and the Law* (Princeton, NJ: Princeton University Press, 1997).

70. Robert W. Bennett and Lawrence B. Solum, *Constitutional Originalism: A Debate* (Ithaca, NY: Cornell University Press, 2011), vii.

71. Edwin Meese III, speech before the D.C. Chapter of the Federalist Society Lawyers Division, November 15, 1985, reprinted in Steven G. Calabresi, ed., *Originalism: A Quarter-Century of Debate* (Washington, DC: Regnery, 2007), 74.

72. Ibid., 79.

73. Steven G. Calabresi, "A Critical Introduction to the Originalism Debate," in Steven G. Calabresi, ed., *Originalism: A Quarter-Century of Debate* (Washington, DC: Regnery, 2007), 4.

74. Antonin Scalia, "Foreword," in Steven G. Calabresi, ed., *Originalism: A Quarter-Century of Debate* (Washington, DC: Regnery, 2007), 43.

75. Jeffrey Toobin, "Heavyweight: How Ruth Bader Ginsburg Has Moved the Supreme Court," *New Yorker*, March 8, 2013, 41.

76. Antonin Scalia, remarks at Woodrow Wilson International Center for Scholars, March 14, 2005, excerpted in George McKenna and Stanley Feingold, eds., *Taking Sides: Clashing Views on Political Issues*, 18th ed. (New York: McGraw-Hill, 2013), 93.

77. Antonin Scalia and Amy Gutmann, *A Matter of Interpretation: Federal Courts and the Law* (Princeton, NJ: Princeton University Press, 1998).

78. Scalia, remarks at Woodrow Wilson Center, 95.

79. Antonin Scalia, William Howard Taft Constitutional Law Lecture, University of Cincinnati, September 16, 1988, reprinted in David M. O'Brien, ed., *Judges on Judging: Views from the Bench*, 3rd ed. (Washington, DC: CQ Press, 2009), 203.

80. William J. Brennan Jr., speech to the Text and Teaching Symposium at Georgetown University, October 12, 1985, reprinted in Steven G. Calabresi, ed., *Originalism: A Quarter-Century of Debate* (Washington, DC: Regnery, 2007), 58–61.

81. Thurgood Marshall, remarks at the annual seminar of the San Francisco Patent and Trademark Law Association, May 16, 1987, reprinted in David M. O'Brien, ed., *Judges on Judging: Views from the Bench*, 3rd ed. (Washington, DC: CQ Press, 2009), 207–208.

82. *Trop v. Dulles*, 356 U.S. 86 at 101 (1958).

83. *Atkins v. Virginia*, 536 U.S. 304 at 321 (2002).

84. *Roper v. Simmons*, 543 U.S. 551 at 561 (2005).

85. *Roper v. Simmons*, 543 U.S. 551 at 587 (2005) (Stevens, J., concurring).

86. Breyer, *Making Democracy Work*, 75.

87. Ibid., 80.

88. Richard A. Posner, *How Judges Think* (Cambridge, MA: Harvard University Press, 2008), 230.

89. Kermit Roosevelt III, *The Myth of Judicial Activism: Making Sense of Supreme Court Decisions* (New Haven: Yale University Press, 2008), 16.

90. Brian Z. Tamanaha, "How an Instrumental View of Law Corrodes the Rule of Law," *DePaul Law Review* 56 (2007): 469–505, at 490.

91. See, e.g., Frank B. Cross, *The Failed Promise of Originalism* (Stanford, CA: Stanford University Press, 2013).

92. See, e.g., Glenn A. Phelps and John B. Gates, "The Myth of Jurisprudence: Interpretive Theory in the Constitutional Opinions of Justices Rehnquist and Brennan," *Santa Clara Law Review* 31 (1991): 567–596; John B. Gates and Glenn A. Phelps, "Intentionalism in Constitutional Opinions," *Political Research Quarterly* 49 (1996): 245–261.

93. Lawrence Baum, *The Puzzle of Judicial Behavior* (Ann Arbor: University of Michigan Press, 1997), 75.

94. Roosevelt, *The Myth of Judicial Activism*.

95. Stefanie A. Lindquist and Frank B. Cross, *Measuring Judicial Activism* (New York: Oxford University Press, 2009), 1.

96. William G. Ross, *A Muted Fury: Populists, Progressives, and Labor Unions Confront the Courts, 1890–1937* (Princeton, NJ: Princeton University Press, 1994).

97. Lucas A. Powe Jr., *The Warren Court and American Politics* (Cambridge, MA: Belknap Press, 2000).

98. See, e.g., Herman Schwartz, ed., *The Rehnquist Court: Judicial Activism on the Right* (New York: Hill and Wang, 2002).

99. Thomas Keck, *The Most Activist Supreme Court in History: The Road to Modern Judicial Conservatism* (Chicago: University of Chicago Press, 2004).

100. David G. Savage, "GOP Lawyers See Tilt to Activist High Court," *Los Angeles Times,* April 1, 2012.

101. Adam Cohen, "Psst ... Justice Scalia ... You Know, You're an Activist Judge Too," *New York Times,* April 19, 2005.

102. Theda Skocpol and Vanessa Williamson, *The Tea Party and the Remaking of Republican Conservatism* (New York: Oxford University Press, 2012), 48.

103. Ibid., 52.

104. Roy B. Flemming, B. Dan Wood, and John Bohte, "Attention to Issues in a System of Separated Powers: The Macrodynamics of American Policy Agendas," *Journal of Politics* 61 (1999): 76–108, at 104.

105. Jonathan D. Casper, "The Supreme Court and National Policy Making," *American Political Science Review* 70 (1976): 50–63, at 62.

106. Ruth Bader Ginsburg, "Communicating and Commenting on the Court's Work," *Georgetown Law Journal* 83 (1995): 2119–2129, at 2125.

107. Robert H. Jackson, *The Supreme Court in the American System of Government* (Cambridge, MA: Harvard University Press, 1955), 2.

108. Quoted in Mark C. Miller, *The View of the Courts from the Hill: Interactions Between Congress and the Federal Judiciary* (Charlottesville: University of Virginia Press, 2009), 8.

Freedoms
The Enactment and Meaning of the Bill of Rights

Michael Stokes Paulsen and Luke Paulsen

AMERICA'S "BILL OF RIGHTS"—THE TITLE TRADITIONALLY attached to the first ten amendments to the US Constitution—is practically a second constitution all its own. This package of amendments was proposed by the First Congress in 1789 and ratified by the states in 1791—just two years after the original Constitution took effect—in the dramatic first exercise of Article V of the Constitution, the article that sets forth the process for amending the Constitution. Hot on the heels of the original document, the Bill of Rights simultaneously completed and made possible the founders' project of radical constitutional overhaul.

Yet the Bill of Rights is in many ways rather traditional. The amendments set forth some of the most cherished liberties of the people: the freedoms of religion, speech, press, and petition; the right to bear arms; the freedom from military intrusion into one's home; the freedom from unreasonable searches and seizures; and the rights of an accused to receive due process and a trial by jury, to confront his or her accusers and present evidence in his or her own favor, not to be tried twice for the same crime, and not to suffer cruel and unusual punishment. These rights, many of which had roots as far back in English history as the Magna Carta of 1215, were designed to serve as specific, absolutely inviolable *written* limitations on the powers of the new national government.

By designing a constitutional structure of separation of powers and federalism, the framers had created a system of checks and balances in the exercise of the new government's powers. The Bill of Rights went further yet: it added an entirely new, comprehensive level of checks on *all* the powers created by the Constitution. In addition, the amendments reaffirmed the principle that the federal government would have only specifically enumerated powers and would have no general power over individual rights. It is thus only a slight exaggeration to say that the adoption of the Bill of Rights was the adoption of a *second constitution*—or perhaps a "second half" to the original Constitution.

The Magna Carta and the English Bill of Rights

For centuries before the US Constitution and Bill of Rights were written, England's Magna Carta ("Great Charter") stood as the greatest example of limitation on arbitrary government. Written in Latin and never fully given effect, the Charter—a list of sixty-one restrictions on royal power—was originally composed in 1215 by rebellious English barons, who forced King John I to agree to it as a condition for peace. Although John later put down the rebellion and rejected the agreement, his successors reissued the Charter in toned-down form as a compromise to keep the peace. The Charter was essentially an agreement between the King and the nobles, but it established the principles of limiting government powers and protecting individual rights, and it remains a potent symbol of these principles today.

The English Bill of Rights—written in 1689 after another revolt against royal authority— went even further in declaring the "rights of Englishmen." Agreed to by England's new rulers (William and Mary) and later made law as an act of Parliament, it established a number of rights held by English citizens as against the monarchy: freedom from royal taxation, freedom to petition the monarch, freedom to bear arms, freedom from a standing army, freedom to elect representatives, freedom of speech, and others. Perhaps even more importantly—at least from a historical point of view—the Bill was a step in the direction of parliamentary supremacy, beginning England's transition to the republican system of government that would, in time, inspire the US Constitution.

In one sense, the American Revolution can be viewed as an act of "constitutional interpretation"—an argument, by the American colonies, that Britain was violating the colonists' rights as Englishmen, as set forth in the Magna Carta and the English Bill of Rights. Much of the Declaration of Independence is a long catalog of charges that the King had irremediably violated Americans' constitutional rights under English tradition.

Both the Magna Carta and the English Bill of Rights were important sources for the US Constitution's Bill of Rights: in particular, most of the ideas behind the First, Second, Third, and Fifth Amendments appear in these documents. But the rights conferred by the English documents worked differently. England did not have a written constitution as such; these documents formed part of the traditional, small-c *constitutional practice* of England. Moreover, many of the rights listed concerned the division of power within the English government—giving Parliament more power and the King less—rather than the protection of individuals from *all* branches of government. America's Bill of Rights thus represented something of a new development—a check from outside the Constitution's structure of representative government and checks and balances, operating directly as supreme law by force of the will of "We the People."

It may even be fair to say that the adoption of the Bill of Rights *saved the Constitution itself.* These amendments quickly calmed the fears of (most) initial opponents of the Constitution that the new government's powers could be used to violate the liberties of the people. As noted in Chapter 1, the adoption of the Bill of Rights helped avert the possibility of a second constitutional convention, thus preserving the achievement of the Philadelphia convention. In effect, the Bill of Rights secured the revolution accomplished by the Constitution by securing the support of the people and confirming the overall constitutional design of broadly worded powers held in check by specific written limitations.

The enduring value of the Bill of Rights lies in its protections of some of the most important freedoms of the American constitutional system. The Bill, originally designed to limit only the power of the new *national* government, quickly became America's credo of liberty, and eventually—after the Civil War—was incorporated by reference in the Fourteenth Amendment's limitations on *state* governments' power as well: "No State shall abridge the privileges or immunities of citizens of the United States. ..." We will discuss the extension of these protections under the Fourteenth Amendment in Chapter 8; here we describe the first ten amendments limiting the national government—the "Bill of Rights" proper.

The Anti-Federalists' Objection and the Federalists' Response

The story of how the Bill of Rights came to be adopted is intertwined with the story of how the Constitution almost was *not* adopted, and merits its own telling. As briefly noted in Chapter 1, the absence of a bill of rights nearly doomed the Constitution. Just five days before the Constitutional Convention ended—after having deliberated for nearly four months—George Mason of Virginia and Elbridge Gerry of Massachusetts pointed out the absence of a bill of rights as a grave defect in the nearly finished draft. How could a plan providing for such sweeping powers in a new central government not contain a declaration of those most basic rights of citizens that the government could never abridge or deny?

Despite these concerns, the convention voted down the suggestion of appointing a group to draft a bill of rights, and the Constitution was sent forward for ratification without such a declaration. Mason, Gerry, and Edmund Randolph of Virginia all felt that this was a serious mistake. Even though they had been part of the drafting of the Constitution all along, they refused to sign the final document in the last days at Philadelphia, in part because it lacked a bill of rights and in part for the closely related reason that they feared that the new national government would be too powerful and overbearing in its authority.

Mason and Gerry soon became prominent leaders of the so-called "Anti-Federalist" opposition to ratification of the Constitution. (Randolph, the third nonsigner, eventually changed his mind and supported ratification.) Joined by other well-known figures—like Patrick Henry of Virginia—Mason, Gerry, and other Anti-Federalists emphasized the Constitution's lack of protection of individual and state rights against a powerful central government as the most important reasons to reject the Constitution.

"Federalist" defenders of the Constitution like James Wilson of Pennsylvania, and Alexander Hamilton writing in *The Federalist* No. 84, responded to these objections with two main arguments. First, they said, a bill of rights was not necessary in a Constitution that granted only limited, specifically delegated powers. Congress, the President, and the courts could only do what the Constitution said they could do, and nothing more. There was no need for a bill of rights to put limits on what the government already lacked the power to do. The national government would have no power to infringe the freedom of speech, or of the press, or the right to jury trial, because no such power was granted anywhere in the Constitution.

Second, the Federalists continued, a bill of rights would actually be *dangerous*. It might be taken to imply that the government actually had broader powers than those set forth in the Constitution, and therefore might *not* be limited to those granted. Moreover, including a bill of rights might be taken as suggesting that the government had the power to restrict all *other* rights of the people—those *not* included in the list of rights. It might be impossible to reach national agreement on what a bill of rights would include, and rights might not be as broadly protected as they were in the various state constitutions and bills of rights. The worst outcome of all would be to adopt a bill of rights that accidentally *narrowed* people's rights and *broadened* government's powers.

So the Federalist argument went. It was slick and sophisticated—but flawed. And the Anti-Federalists had some persuasive responses. To be sure, the national government was *in theory* one of limited, delegated powers, they said. But look at how broad those "limited" powers were: the Constitution granted power to Congress and the President in truly sweeping terms (as we have seen in Chapter 3). For instance, the power to regulate commerce, the power to impose taxes, and the power to pass laws "necessary and proper" for carrying into effect all powers granted to any branch of the national government were huge powers. Each might be employed in such a way as to affect basic rights. Who needs a specific power to regulate the press, for example, if the government might have the power to regulate "commerce" (including the press) or to pass laws "necessary and proper" to carry into execution the nation's war power (including suppressing speech or publications considered harmful to the nation's security)? Could not those be used in such a way as to restrict the press's freedom to publish? If a "necessary and proper" law for carrying into effect a regulation of commerce might include criminal prosecution and punishments for those who violated the law, should not the right to trial by jury be protected?

The examples went on and on. Besides, the Anti-Federalists argued, why not be especially cautious? Would it really be so hard to write a bill of rights, based on state examples? What was the problem? As Patrick Henry caustically quipped, would it have taken too much paper? The Anti-Federalists also scoffed at the argument that a bill of rights would be dangerous. The Constitution already had some specific provisions protecting individual rights: it prohibited "bills of attainder" (laws simply declaring someone to be a criminal) and "ex post facto" laws (making it a crime to have done something in the past that was not a crime at the time the thing was done). Did those provisions somehow imply that the national government had broader powers, or power to control all rights?

Besides, the Anti-Federalists argued, why not just try to write as good a bill of rights as possible and then add further provisions saying that such a list should in no way imply that other rights, like state bills of rights, were thereby taken away or assigned into the hands of the national government? And if anyone was really concerned that such a bill of rights would be misinterpreted as implying that the national government was *not* one of limited powers, why not just include another amendment reaffirming that this was not so? How hard was it, really? (As we shall see, these suggestions eventually became the basis for the Ninth Amendment and the Tenth Amendment, respectively—amendments that perfectly countered the Federalists' objections to a bill of rights.)

The Federalists were forced to back off. It is sometimes said that the Federalists gave us the Constitution and the Anti-Federalists gave us the Bill of Rights. This is not a bad shorthand description, but it is not quite the complete picture. Some Anti-Federalists used the lack of a bill of rights as a pretext for trying to kill the Constitution entirely, because they preferred to leave things the way they were with power centered in their state governments. For them, getting a bill of rights added to the Constitution was not really the objective; defeating the Constitution was. Other Anti-Federalists wanted a second constitutional convention, with a bill of rights and other changes made *before* they would vote for ratification. Still others liked the Constitution for the most part, but wanted assurances that a bill of rights would be added promptly once the new Constitution was adopted.

Once again it was James Madison who rose to the occasion, playing the most prominent role in writing the Bill of Rights. Madison recognized the fairness of the Anti-Federalists' argument for a bill of rights, even though he did not entirely agree with it. Madison led the Federalists in agreeing to propose a bill of rights as one of the first items of business in the new Congress. But ratification of the Constitution must come first, the Federalists insisted. They did not want a second constitutional convention where the delicate compromises at Philadelphia might be revisited. That would risk the entire enterprise unraveling. As we saw in Chapter 1, the agreement to propose a bill of rights took the best argument away from opponents of the Constitution and took the steam out of their efforts to defeat it. By agreeing to sponsor a bill of rights, the Federalists divided—and conquered—the Anti-Federalist opposition.

In the end, therefore, credit for the Bill of Rights must be shared. It was James Madison and other supporters of the Constitution—men who had originally opposed having a bill of rights, on the theory that it was unnecessary and dangerous—who ended up proposing the bill of rights. But they did so in part because of political pressure from Anti-Federalists— some of whom wanted the Constitution killed more than they wanted a bill of rights added. The Anti-Federalists prodded; the Federalists produced.

But Madison and the Federalists did not produce exactly what the Anti-Federalists wanted. The Anti-Federalists did not merely want specific individual rights protected; they wanted the powers of the new national government curtailed. In particular, they wanted new language similar to that in the old Articles of Confederation, limiting the central government to the exercise of those powers *expressly* delegated and leaving all else to the states. Madison would not retreat that far from the Constitution's original vision. Instead, when he took office as a member of the House of Representatives in the First Congress in 1789, he made good on the Federalists' promise of a bill of rights, but cast the proposals in his own terms. To be sure, they included broad protections for individual liberties, but they also reaffirmed the principle of enumerated powers *without* the addition of the word "expressly" attached as a limitation. The ironic effect was to preserve and arguably strengthen the original framework of a national government of enumerated—but still broadly worded—powers. The check would come only from the specific protections of individual rights.

Article V: The Amendment Process

Article V of the Constitution lays out an elaborate obstacle course for amending the Constitution, specifying two alternative paths for changing the document. Under the first, a proposed amendment must first pass Congress with the support of at least two-thirds of the members of each house. Then it must be ratified by three-fourths of the states, either by special ratifying conventions (the way the original Constitution was approved) or by state legislatures—whichever method Congress chooses.

Article V's alternative route for amending the Constitution has never (yet) been used: if two-thirds of the states' legislatures so request, Congress must call a constitutional convention for proposing amendments; those proposals then must be ratified by three-fourths of the states, just as with amendments proposed by Congress. Again, Congress chooses whether states will ratify using special conventions or through their state legislatures.

The first procedure allows Congress to draft specific proposed amendments, giving it some measure of control over change. In contrast, a constitutional convention could propose whatever it wished, free from any other elected officials' control, leading some to fear a "runaway" constitutional convention that could end up proposing an entirely new constitution. (After all, isn't that what the Philadelphia convention did in 1787?) But a convention could only *propose* amendments; three-fourths of the states would need to ratify any proposal, just as with congressionally proposed amendments.

Why has there never been a convention for proposing amendments? At one point in the 1990s, more than two-thirds of the states had submitted to Congress calls for a constitutional convention. Even setting aside those that called for a convention only if "limited" to a certain topic (an arrangement probably not permitted by Article V), there were still sufficient state applications requesting a *general* convention to satisfy Article V's two-thirds threshold. Congress may well have been under an (overlooked!) obligation to call a constitutional convention. Since then, some states have withdrawn their convention applications. The number of states that have requested a convention continues to hover just shy of the magic number of thirty-four, meaning that a second constitutional convention remains a very real possibility for the modern era.

Not all of Madison's proposals achieved the two-thirds majorities of both houses of Congress needed to become constitutional amendment proposals sent to the states. Indeed, one further irony was that Madison proposed certain individual-rights limitations on what *state* governments could do—a concern of his, but not a concern of Anti-Federalists. That proposal of Madison's went nowhere, and did not emerge from Congress. What emerged instead, after much debate and modification in both the House and the Senate, were *twelve* constitutional amendments that limited the federal government only, including the ten we know today as the Bill of Rights. We now turn to those first ten amendments.

The First Amendment: Freedom for Religion, Speech, and Press

The First Amendment to the Constitution is a compendium of some of the most treasured freedoms of America—freedom of religion, freedom of speech, freedom of the press, and freedom of assembly and petition. All, in some sense, are freedoms of the mind, will, and heart. The amendment reads in full:

> Congress shall make no law respecting an establishment of religion, or prohibiting the free exercise thereof; or abridging the freedom of speech, or of the press; or the right of the people peaceably to assemble, and to petition the Government for a redress of grievances.

We begin where the Bill of Rights begins: religious liberty. The quest for religious freedom was one of the major reasons why many people came to America in the first place. Religious faith was then, and remains, of greatest importance for the lives, values, and worldviews of many Americans. The First Amendment reflects and embraces that importance, protecting not merely freedom of religious *belief* (or "conscience") but the "free *exercise*" of religion—the right to live out one's faith, to act in accordance with what God requires even if this might sometimes conflict with what the state otherwise commands through its laws.

The Case of the Missing Amendments

The first Congress proposed twelve amendments. The states ratified just ten by 1791. What happened to the other two? Neither was ratified at the time of the other proposals. The first of the two rejected amendments was a complicated, confusing, badly worded proposal that would have increased the total size of the House of Representatives. The proposed amendment fell one vote short of ratification. The margin of defeat was supplied by tiny Delaware, which would have seen its relative weight in the House of Representatives diminished had the proposal been adopted.

The second proposed amendment was a limitation on the ability of Congress to vote itself salary increases. This proposal has perhaps the most unusual history of any proposed constitutional amendment. It reads as follows:

> No law, varying the compensation for the services of the Senators and Representatives, shall take effect, until an election of Representatives shall have intervened.

The idea was that if Congress voted itself too high a pay raise, it might never take effect; the people might overrule their decision by electing new representatives and senators. But when this amendment was first proposed by Congress in 1789, it received only six state ratifications, well short of the three-fourths needed.

But take a look at the very end of the Constitution: the Congressional Pay Amendment *was* ratified by the states—in *1992,* more than 200 years after it had been proposed by the First Congress. The amendment proposal lay dormant—and presumed dead—until the 1980s and 1990s, when state legislatures caught on to the idea that the amendment might yet be ratified. Many people had become frustrated with Congress repeatedly voting itself pay raises. The movement to ratify the amendment caught fire, and in May 1992, Michigan—which was not even a state in 1789—became the thirty-eighth state to ratify, making a three-fourths majority. The Congressional Pay Amendment, originally proposed to be the second amendment, is now the Twenty-Seventh Amendment to the Constitution.

The founding generation, as a rule, believed that God exists; that God may make demands upon human conduct; that the commands of God precede and are superior in obligation to any rules adopted by mere human society; and that government was incompetent to decide which religious beliefs were true and which were false, or to command which should be obeyed and which should be overruled by society's laws. The right to the free exercise of religion was therefore an inalienable "natural right" that preceded the Constitution and the social compact, a sphere that no mere human authority could properly invade. That was why James Madison worried aloud, when introducing his proposed Bill of Rights in the House of Representatives, that liberties like religious freedom not be set forth in language too narrow, as if to suggest that they were *granted* by the Constitution rather than *recognized* in the Constitution. The right to the free exercise of religion was not properly subject to man's definition and control, under any system of government.

The First Amendment's wording thus represented a dramatic expansion and improvement upon earlier notions of religious freedom, which frequently spoke in terms of "toleration" of religion. In America, religion is not merely to be *tolerated;* it is to be *respected, accommodated,* and *protected* as a fundamental, inalienable, (literally) God-given natural right that government may never infringe.

The First Amendment protects religious freedom in two distinct but related ways—approaching the same broad value from two different directions. First, it prohibits the national government from setting up an "establishment" of religion—a state-sponsored church or official religion. The core purpose of the Establishment Clause was to prohibit the new national government from establishing an official religion and requiring everyone to belong to it, adhere to its tenets, or support it with special taxes. In America, government may impose no punishment, penalty, or discrimination based on a person's religious exercise *or lack thereof.* The essence of the Establishment Clause is that government may not use compulsion or coercion, in any form, to make someone engage in religious exercise other than in accordance with his or her own free choice.

The Establishment Clause originally had a second purpose: to forbid the national government from *dis*-establishing official *state* government churches, of which there were many at the time. (The famously long word "antidisestablishmentarianism" has a real meaning, referring to those who *opposed discontinuing* official state religions.) The Establishment Clause meant that the national government was to have no power to establish a national religion or to interfere with state establishments; it was to stay out of the business altogether. Ironically, the intent was to protect states' rights to have official state religions. Today no state has an established church. Moreover, as noted earlier in this chapter, the Fourteenth Amendment, adopted in 1868, applied the Bill of Rights to state governments, so that today neither the federal government nor the states may have established churches or compel people to engage in religious practices against their will.

The second way in which the First Amendment protects religious liberty is that it forbids government from prohibiting the "free exercise" of religion: The Free Exercise Clause means that government may not punish, penalize, or discriminate against the exercise of religion in any way. This means more than just tolerating religion; government must honor its *free*—unpenalized and unburdened—*exercise*. It may not inhibit the ability to put one's religious beliefs into action.

The Establishment Clause and the Free Exercise Clause thus can be seen as two sides of the same coin. Non-establishment means that government cannot *make* someone exercise religion through its power to coerce or punish; and free exercise means that government cannot *keep* someone from exercising religion, even if this may mean departing from its usual rules in order to permit individuals and groups freely to exercise their religious beliefs.

For more than two centuries, scholars and judges have argued about how broad the right to the free exercise of religion is. Can it really mean that some people's religious beliefs may exempt them from laws that apply to everyone else? What if their religious beliefs lead them to engage in drug use, or polygamy, or ritual human sacrifice? Can freedom of religion really mean so much?

As we shall see in later chapters, the Supreme Court has waffled back and forth over time on the meaning of the First Amendment's freedoms for religion. For many years, it protected the free exercise of religion to the broadest extent possible, siding with persons exercising this freedom except in cases where it would present clear harm or danger to others. But in more recent years, the Supreme Court has said that if a law is "neutral" in form—if it does not specifically mention or target religious practice—it usually does not violate the Free Exercise Clause, even if its effect is to keep some people from freely exercising their religion. That position is troubling too: what if government passed a law requiring workers to be available to work for employers on every day of the week or else suffer some sort of financial penalty—even though this might conflict, for many people, with a religious obligation to "[h]onor the Sabbath and keep it holy" by not working one day a week, typically either Saturday or Sunday? (This question was posed by a real case—in fact, several of them—addressed by the Supreme Court in the twentieth century.) Such a law is "neutral" in one sense: it treats everyone in the same way. But the law also clearly has the effect of punishing or prohibiting the free observance of religious faith.

Formal neutrality is often not enough to protect the free exercise of religion. As many have pointed out, the very fact that the First Amendment protects the free exercise of religion means that the Constitution is *not* neutral with respect to religion. It gives religious belief and exercise special protection from government.

An even more basic riddle: what is "religion" within the meaning of the First Amendment? Clearly, it does not refer to just *anything* an individual believes. Rather, for the framers, "religion" meant some form of a *belief in God (or gods) and the duties that come from such beliefs.* The reason for protecting religious freedom was, as noted, the idea that one's duties to God are higher than one's duties to the state and that government must respect that. That did not mean the framers thought that all religious beliefs were equally *true*; it simply meant the framers thought they should all be equally *free*. Precisely because religion was so important, it was something that could not be entrusted to the power of government. But religious beliefs needed to be truly *religious*—some form of belief in a God (or gods), not merely an individual's personal beliefs or personal philosophy of life. The commands of God may trump the commands of the state, but individuals cannot make *themselves* "God" and make their own commands superior to the laws of society.

Next after religious freedom, the First Amendment protects *"the freedom of speech."* Freedom of speech was valued by the framing generation almost as highly as freedom of religion, but for different reasons. Freedom of expression was valued perhaps less for its own sake (as religion generally was) than for its instrumental function of checking government. The right to criticize the government—to organize opposition to its policies—to advocate change—was viewed by the framers as essential to the working of free, democratic government. Thus, even when such criticism or opposition was unfair, unjustified, or even seemingly irresponsible, the right to express such views had to be protected. Government power to restrict the freedom of speech would be far worse than allowing "bad" speech. The right to criticize government and to express one's views freely on any subject was understood at the time of the adoption of the First Amendment to be *the* single best protection against government tyranny that a free society could have. And it remains so today.

Likewise, *"the freedom of the press"* protects the right to publish and distribute one's views in written form, without government censorship. This may permit a lot of garbage to be printed or published; but it also permits criticism, critique, inquiry, and argument about matters of politics, policy, and much else. The freedoms of speech and of the press are central features of a free society; suppression, censorship, and state control are the hallmarks of despotic regimes.

The Speech and Press clauses, expressed in the leanest of language, logically entail a number of vital principles. "Speech," under the First Amendment, includes more than spoken words. It can include symbolic expression and even some forms of action meant to express a message. Burning a flag, marching in protest, wearing a black armband—all are forms of "speech." (These examples all come from free speech cases in the modern era, as we will see in later chapters.) Likewise, "the press" covers all media of written, published, or broadcast expression: television, radio, movies, the Internet, and more. Between the two of them, these companion freedoms—speech and press—protect essentially all forms of verbal, symbolic, and written expression. Though the framers certainly did not anticipate all the applications to which the freedoms of speech and press would be put, or the technological developments that would provide new forms and means of communication, the meaning of the words they used in the First Amendment certainly embraces such situations.

The core of both provisions is simply this: *Government may not prohibit, punish, or penalize the expression of views (whether spoken or written) on account of the ideas, message, content, or viewpoint being expressed*. This is an important point. The very essence of the First Amendment's protection of speech and press is that government does not get to control what people say or write. (As we shall see, however, this principle has been violated on more than one occasion in our nation's history.)

There are certain exceptions to this principle. First, as a matter of the historical understanding of the First Amendment's terms, not all things that might be classified as "speech" are covered by "*the freedom of*" speech. Obscene, sexually explicit material is generally not protected. Neither are false advertising, false statements about other people ("defamation"), "threats," direct incitements to immediate illegal or violent acts, or other false statements harmful to others. The classic example, from the 1919 Supreme Court case *Schenck v. United States*, is "falsely shouting fire in a theatre and causing a panic." Moreover, even though the First Amendment is written in absolute terms, certain compelling reasons have long been recognized as justifying narrowly tailored limitations on freedom of speech and press. Here, the classic example (from the 1931 case of *Near v. Minnesota*) is a newspaper publishing a vital national security secret during time of war, such as where American troop ships will be heading for a battle with the enemy.

In addition, nothing in the amendment prevents government from regulating *conduct*—actions—as long as it is not regulating conduct *because of any speech-message involved*. For example, government may make it illegal to set unauthorized fires in public places. That is a straightforward regulation of actions. But it may not make it illegal specifically to burn a flag or a draft card *as an act of public protest*. In short, government can ban fires, but not protests. If it bans fires because they are protest fires, it is really targeting the speech-message, not the conduct.

Finally, government does not "abridge" the freedom of speech where it merely regulates the time, place, or manner of speech—again, as long as this is not a disguise for restricting speech because of its message. Thus, government may deny a parade permit to make sure that two parades are not going down the street at the same time, running into each other. But it may not deny a parade permit because it dislikes a group's message or fears it will offend onlookers. Similarly, government may prohibit the use of bullhorns in residential neighborhoods in the middle of the night—not to censor the speaker's message, but to let people sleep.

Some Burning Controversies Over the Freedom of Speech

The freedom of speech logically applies to *symbolic* speech as well—the use of symbols, flags, and images that have meaning and communicate ideas. But not every action of government that affects symbolic expression necessarily "abridge[s] the freedom of speech." The line is well illustrated by several modern classic Supreme Court decisions concerning people setting fire to certain objects for expressive purposes.

In *United States v. O'Brien* (1968), the Supreme Court held that government could punish the act of burning a draft card—an official government notice of a person's eligibility to be drafted for mandatory military service—as long as the government's law was not aimed at the act of protest but applied *any* time a person deliberately destroyed, altered, or mutilated such a document, for any reason. Mr. O'Brien's political and rhetorical motives were irrelevant. What mattered was that the government's law was addressed to *conduct,* pure and simple, and *not* to any expressive message the draft-card-burner wished to convey.

In a contrasting famous case, *Texas v. Johnson* (1989), the Court held that burning an American flag in protest was symbolic expression protected by the First Amendment. Texas had a law that prohibited flag "desecration," including burning a flag in protest. The Court contrasted this situation with the law at issue in *O'Brien.* While government generally may enact laws to punish conduct it thinks improper, it may not punish expressive conduct *because of* its expressive message or content. The Court found that the protester was not prosecuted for setting fires, but because of the message conveyed by the fact that it was the US flag that had been set afire. However offensive this symbolic act might be, government could no more punish it because of its offensiveness than it could punish an offensive speech. The close decision in *Texas v. Johnson* (5–4) set off a firestorm of criticism, including efforts to amend the Constitution specifically to protect the American flag. So far, those efforts have not been successful.

The First Amendment often serves to protect offensive speakers and messages. For example, two famous—and unanimous—decisions have upheld the rights of Ku Klux Klan cross-burners: *R.A.V. v. City of St. Paul* (1992) and *Brandenburg v. Ohio* (1969). The amendment protects the expression of even hateful ideas. Other cases have sided with neo-Nazi groups wishing to parade through the streets of a town full of Holocaust survivors, and with purveyors of pornographic, degrading images of women. Such decisions are generally considered the (regrettable) price of freedom of speech—a right so valued in other respects.

For much more on freedom of speech controversies in American constitutional history, see Chapters 8, 9, and 10.

It is sometimes said that the First Amendment also protects the freedom "of association" in addition to the freedoms of speech and press. While not set out on its own terms, the right to associate with others to engage in expressive activity is implicit in the fact that every individual possesses these rights and may choose to exercise them in combination with like-minded fellow citizens. Thus, the "freedom of expressive association" allows groups to form, without government interference, around distinctive views and messages. Another, related aspect of the freedom of speech is that government may not compel individuals or groups to express messages they do not wish to convey; the private speaker or group—never the government—gets to control the content of the expression.

Adhering to the requirements of the First Amendment freedoms of speech and the press sometimes proves difficult, as it often requires giving constitutional protection to the expression of views that many find offensive, hateful, evil, or just plain stupid. And the courts have not always proved equal to the task, as we shall see in later chapters. But for the most part, the freedoms of speech and the press—and the related First Amendment rights to assemble and petition the government for redress of grievances—have succeeded, as the framers intended, in safeguarding rights that also serve as vital checks on government power.

The Second and Third Amendments

The Second Amendment, which protects the right to "keep and bear arms," is the only one that comes with a statement of purpose:

> A well-regulated Militia, being necessary to the security of a free State, the right of the people to keep and bear Arms, shall not be infringed.

A "Militia" was understood at the time to be all able-bodied men capable of bearing firearms to protect the community. Picture the "Minutemen" of the early days of the Revolutionary War, ready on a moment's notice when summoned by Paul Revere in April 1775 to engage the British army at Lexington and Concord in Massachusetts.

Such memories were still fresh in the public mind when the Constitution was adopted. Many feared that an American "standing army" might become a threat to liberty, like the British forces that had bullied and intimidated the colonists in the years leading up to the American Revolution. This same concern was at the heart of the Third Amendment (in some ways a close cousin of the Second), which forbids a standing army from taking over people's homes:

> No Soldier shall, in time of peace be quartered in any house, without the consent of the Owner, nor in time of war, but in a manner to be prescribed by law.

A professional military must not be permitted to oppress the people, as the British army did when "quartered" in American cities before and during the Revolution. Rather, the people must have the right to the freedom of their homes against military occupation.

The Third Amendment was simply a declaration of the right to the privacy of one's home, as against a standing army. The Second Amendment packed more of a punch. Part of its purpose was to enable local militias—the people bearing arms—to serve as a potential *military* "check" against the potential tyranny of a national army, if it were ever improperly turned against the people's liberty by some usurping dictator. This idea may seem surprising (and unlikely) today, but the goal of the amendment was to check national military power with the power of the people to keep and bear arms to protect their communities—and their families—from *whatever* might threaten their safety or liberty.

James Madison and Alexander Hamilton had expressed the same idea in *The Federalist* just a few years earlier: "[A] militia amounting to near half a million of citizens with arms in their hands," with the help of state and local governments, could always defeat a national army that improperly tried to seize power, Madison wrote in *The Federalist* No. 46, reminding readers of the "late successful resistance of this country against the British arms." The Constitution's division of power between state and national governments would also help, by enabling the states to organize resistance against potential tyrants: "Besides the advantage of being armed, which the Americans possess over the people of almost every other nation, the existence of subordinate governments, to which the people are attached and by which the militia officers are appointed, forms a barrier against the enterprises of ambition, more insurmountable than any which a simple government of any form can admit of." Despite these reassurances, Anti-Federalists wanted this power of the people expressly preserved. The Second Amendment did so in dramatic fashion, by protecting a constitutional right of individual citizens to keep and bear arms.

The Second Amendment presents some fascinating questions of interpretation. What are the limits of this right? Is it subject to government restriction, since the amendment speaks of the purpose of a "well-regulated" militia? Or would such restrictions defeat its whole purpose of enabling the armed citizenry to check government? If the right is one that belongs to each individual, can it be used for individual safety as well as community safety? And just what does the amendment mean by "arms"? Certainly, individuals have no right to own their own nuclear missiles or rocket launchers, do they? On the other hand, the right to bear arms can no more be limited to colonial-era muskets and exclude today's rifles and handguns than the freedom of the press can be limited to old-style printing presses and exclude websites. A constitutional right does not vanish just because of changes in technology. Does it vanish because Americans are more trusting of the military today, so that the original reasons for the amendment seem less pressing?

These are just a few of the troubling issues surrounding the interpretation of [the] Second Amendment. The amendment remains hotly debated, generating strong opposing views, about which the courts have reached surprisingly few settled answers. Indeed, it was not until 2008 that the Supreme Court issued its first major interpretation of the amendment, in *District of Columbia v. Heller*. In a closely divided (5–4) holding, the Court found that the right to "keep and bear arms" includes a right of personal gun possession; the "militia" clause preamble described the framers' historical *purpose* for including this right in the Bill of Rights, but did not limit the right itself. In a subsequent case decided in 2010 (*McDonald v. City of Chicago*), the Court, again by a vote of 5–4, held that the right to keep and bear arms also applied against state and local governments, by virtue of the Fourteenth Amendment. Among the issues left open by the *Heller* and *McDonald* decisions, however, were what *kinds* of weapons an individual has a Second Amendment right to own, what restrictions government may place on *who* can own handguns (such as former felons or the mentally ill), and what procedural restrictions concerning registration, regulation, and training a state may impose. These questions remain the subject of much legitimate debate, the lines of disagreement often reflecting divisions over the merits of the Second Amendment itself, as well as its interpretation.

The Fourth Amendment

The Fourth Amendment provides:

> The right of the people to be secure in their persons, houses, papers, and effects, against unreasonable searches and seizures, shall not be violated, and no Warrants shall issue, but upon probable cause, supported by Oath or affirmation, and particularly describing the place to be searched, and the persons or things to be seized.

The Fourth Amendment owes its roots in part to the history of American colonial smuggling to avoid British taxes on certain goods, in the years leading up to the American Revolution. Colonists were outraged over arbitrary searches of their homes and businesses by British officials looking for smuggled goods. Frequently, such searches were authorized by "General Warrants"—blanket authorizations for crown or colonial officials to search wherever they wished and seize whatever they thought appropriate. The Declaration of Independence lists such intrusions as among the reasons justifying the American Revolution. This history goes a long way toward explaining why the Fourth Amendment was included in the Bill of Rights.

The Fourth Amendment forbids "unreasonable searches and seizures" by government officials. In America, government officials may not invade a person's home or business—or arrest someone or seize property as evidence—without good reason. The amendment safeguards the right of the people to be free from such arbitrary government intrusions. If the police have reason to believe that a person may be guilty of a crime or hiding evidence, they may obtain a warrant for that person's arrest or a search warrant to investigate his or her home or business. But the Fourth Amendment says that officials requesting a warrant must show that they have "probable cause" to believe the person has committed a crime or is hiding evidence. In addition, a warrant can only be issued on the basis of a sworn statement by the officials seeking it, "particularly describing the place to be searched, and the persons or things to be seized."

The amendment seeks to strike a balance. It does not forbid *all* searches and seizures, only "unreasonable" ones. It does not say that all searches and seizures require warrants, either. In fact, the amendment was designed in part to *limit* the use of warrants, which had been abused by the British government in colonial times.

Without a warrant, arresting someone or entering someone's home without permission may violate that person's legal rights, even if he or she turns out to be guilty of a crime. If the police did not have a warrant, and if their actions are later held to be "unreasonable," the search or seizure was unconstitutional. Originally, this meant that anyone whose home or business was searched, or whose property or person was wrongfully seized, might sue the government official for breaking and entering, or for trespassing, just as they could sue any other person who broke into their home or took their property. A warrant, however, gave the government officials "immunity" from being sued because the warrant gave the officer legal authority to search. That is part of the reason the Fourth Amendment sought to limit warrants to situations where police had "probable cause" to believe that evidence of crime would be found. Without a warrant, police would have to act with even greater care to make sure their conduct was "reasonable." If it was not, a jury might later award "damages"—monetary compensation—to someone whose rights were violated by unreasonable actions of government officials, and make the offending officials pay. The idea was to deter unjustified searches and seizures and to compensate people when their rights were violated.

More recently, courts have often excluded evidence obtained in violation of the Fourth Amendment from a criminal trial. This modern "exclusionary rule" remains controversial because it has a high cost: a guilty criminal may go free because of a blunder by the police. Meanwhile, the innocent citizen who is subjected to an illegal search has no real remedy. The Fourth Amendment itself does not say what the remedy should be when the amendment is violated. It does not say that evidence of a crime should be excluded from trial. Yet, as we shall see in Chapter 10, the Supreme Court established the exclusionary rule in 1960 and has stuck with it ever since, on the theory that it serves to deter police from engaging in unreasonable searches and encourages them to obtain warrants whenever possible.

The Fifth, Sixth, Seventh, and Eighth Amendments

The Fifth, Sixth, Seventh, and Eighth Amendments each concern, in different ways, the right to fair trials and punishments. They contain provisions requiring that trials be in accordance with laws and rules laid down in advance ("due process of law"); protecting a person from being compelled to testify against himself or herself (the privilege against self-incrimination), from being tried or punished twice for the same crime (the "double jeopardy" clause), and from "cruel and unusual punishments" or excessive fines (the Eighth Amendment); assuring the right not to be held without charges or without bail; and guaranteeing the rights to a speedy and public trial, to confront one's accusers, and to have the assistance of a lawyer. Most importantly of all from the standpoint of those who fought for the Bill of Rights, the amendments protect the vital right to "trial by jury."

All of these rights are familiar today. Indeed, most of them were familiar at the time, drawn from state bills of rights and from English traditions dating back hundreds of years. The Fifth, Sixth, Seventh, and Eighth Amendments did not break new ground. They merely made clear that these ancient rights would apply to proceedings in the newly-created national courts.

Two themes tie these amendments together. First, they are all designed *to protect the innocent* against wrongful accusation, trial, or punishment—and even to protect the guilty against unfair procedures and punishments. Government may prosecute and punish persons for crimes, but its process must be fair. Second, the amendments enshrine *the institution of the jury* as an important "check" of the people against government power. These themes go hand in hand: protecting the innocent from false or overblown charges can often be accomplished *because* a jury of ordinary citizens is there to check the government's power.

Note how these amendments tend to safeguard and vindicate innocence. "Due process of law" requires government to observe regular and fair procedures. Criminal offenses must be defined by law, in advance, and government must give notice of all charges and a fair opportunity for the accused to answer them. This was what the Fifth Amendment meant in guaranteeing that no one can be deprived of liberty "without due process of law." As we shall see in the next chapter, the Supreme Court twisted the meaning of this phrase beyond all recognition in one of its worst decisions of all time, the infamous *Dred Scott* case, decided in 1857, finding that the right to *due process* included the substantive right of (white) citizens to *own slaves*, even where Congress had prohibited it. But the proper meaning of "due process" is straightforward and sensible: fair procedures, fair notice, and the rule of laws written in advance and not made up case by case.

The rights set forth in the Sixth Amendment—the rights to the assistance of counsel, to confront one's accusers, and to call witnesses on one's own behalf—are all designed to help an innocent person prove his or her innocence. The right to trial by jury does this too—not just once, but at two different stages of the proceedings. A "grand jury," usually a large group of twenty-four ordinary citizens, must give its consent before the government may bring serious criminal charges. A "petit jury," that is, an ordinary twelve-person "jury of one's peers," must hear the evidence and agree that a defendant is guilty, beyond a reasonable doubt. Thus, it is not up to the government to decide whether a person is guilty. A body of citizens, the jury, stands between the government and the accused. This group of temporary representatives of the people holds the final decision-making power before anyone can be imprisoned for a crime.

The Fifth Amendment protects the right to a grand jury. The Sixth Amendment protects the right to a trial by jury in criminal prosecutions brought by the government. The Seventh Amendment protects the right to a trial by jury in civil cases where the amount in dispute is more than twenty dollars—disputes between two private parties or between a citizen and the government, such as suits to vindicate legal rights the citizen has against the government. The framers thought the right to trial by jury in most civil cases to be as important as the right to a jury in criminal cases. The jury would serve as a vital check on government power—in this instance, on the *judicial* power—in every significant legal case between citizen and government and between citizen and citizen. As Thomas Jefferson put it, with typical verve—and perhaps slight overstatement, for dramatic effect—"Were I called upon to decide whether the people had best be omitted in the Legislative or Judicial department, I would say it is better to leave them out of the Legislative."

It is difficult to exaggerate how greatly the founding generation valued the right to trial by jury, and how much Americans of that era valued the institution of the jury as a way of bringing ordinary people directly into the operation of the law. The jury was understood to be the very bulwark of constitutional liberty precisely because the institution of the jury put the People in charge, ultimately, of the administration of their government. The jury was originally understood as having not only the power to judge the facts of a case, but an independent right to interpret the *law* as well—a power that, taken seriously and applied to the Constitution as supreme law, has profound (and to modern sensibilities, somewhat rattling) implications: it would vest in grand juries, criminal juries, and civil juries a *co-equal province of constitutional interpretation* with judges; the jury would be, in effect, the "lower house" of a bicameral judiciary. This traditional right of the jury to interpret and apply the law in cases before them, independently of the views of the judges, should not be confused with the idea of "jury nullification"—the name sometimes given to the raw power of the jury (defended as legitimate by some) to *disobey* or *defy* the law for political purposes. The founding idea was different: juries had an equal right to judge the law—to interpret and apply it, in good faith—but were bound by oath and conscience to give fair effect to its proper meaning, not simply to ignore the law whenever the members of the jury did not like what it said.

It was the absence of a provision guaranteeing jury trial in civil cases that first provoked delegates George Mason and Elbridge Gerry to insist on a bill of rights near the close of the Constitutional Convention. The Seventh Amendment cured that defect, while the Fifth and Sixth Amendments enhanced jury trial rights in criminal cases.

One provision of the Fifth Amendment at first glance appears to be of a different character than the rest of the amendment, which chiefly concerns fair trial procedures. The Takings Clause—"nor shall private property be taken for public use, without just compensation"—forbids government from simply seizing private property for its own purposes. If government uses the power of "eminent domain" to "condemn" private property for public use (like building a road, school, or post office), it must fairly compensate the owner. If the government and the property owner cannot reach agreement, the amount of compensation is to be determined in a trial by a jury—that central institution, once again, in effect interpreting and judging the meaning of "just compensation" in a particular case.

In recent years, debates over the Takings Clause have focused on three large points. First, what counts as "property"? The Constitution does not define the term, seemingly leaving the definition to state law or the common law. Property generally refers to more than just land or personal property, but to anything an individual might own to the exclusion of others. Whatever is considered property under the governing law, government may not take it without paying just compensation.

Second, what constitutes a "taking" of property? Does it include government *regulation* impairing property's value? The answer is not perfectly clear, and modern courts have struggled with questions of whether government has physically intruded on property and with the degree to which regulation deprives owners of all economically viable uses of property. That struggle has not produced clear resolution.

Third, what is a "public use"? In a famous modern case, *Kelo v. New London* (2005), the Supreme Court split bitterly, 5–4, over whether a state could seize people's homes against their wills (albeit with monetary compensation) in order to transfer property to a private commercial development. The property owners—including one who had been born in her house in 1918 and had lived there all her life—did not want to move, period. They argued that condemnation of their homes in order to furnish land for a private development was not a *public* use and that the Constitution restricted the power of eminent domain to such uses. The city of New London, Connecticut, argued that the general economic benefits to the community flowing from the development constituted a sufficient "public purpose" for the condemnation. (Interestingly, the Takings Clause does not quite say that government may only take property for a "public use," but only that, *if* property is taken for such a use, *then* compensation is required. Does that mean that government can simply redistribute property from one person to another, without paying compensation, or does the Takings Clause presume that any government taking of property must be for a public use?) The Supreme Court majority sided with the city, adopting the broad "public purpose" argument.

The *Kelo* decision produced a vigorous public backlash, leading more than forty states to adopt state laws providing their citizens with greater protections against takings by local governments. In a sad postscript, the New London development was not entirely successful, and the private company for whose benefit the city had condemned the homeowners' land left the site just a few years later, leaving substantial parts of the land undeveloped and a partial wasteland where Susette Kelo's house had once stood.

The Ninth and Tenth Amendments

The last two amendments traditionally included as part of the Bill of Rights, the Ninth and the Tenth, do not really contain any rights at all. They serve a different purpose: they answer the objections that the Federalists had raised against having a bill of rights in the first place. Recall that the Federalists had argued that a bill of rights would be dangerous in that it might suggest that the Constitution thus *took away* all *other* legal rights that people might have had—for example, citizens' rights under state constitutions, held against their own state governments. Further, by creating "exceptions to powers which are not granted," it might "afford a colorable pretext" (Hamilton's words in *The Federalist* No. 84) for someone to claim *broader* national powers than were given.

As noted earlier, both arguments were a bit strained. But in any event, the Ninth and Tenth Amendments seem perfectly designed to prevent any such improper inferences. The Ninth Amendment explains:

> The enumeration in the Constitution, of certain rights, shall not be construed
> to deny or disparage others retained by the people.

Simply by enumerating certain rights possessed by the American people, the Bill of Rights does not repeal any other rights the people had retained against their own state governments. Nor did it purport to repeal the "natural law" rights of all men and women, including the ultimate right of the people, exercised first by America in the Declaration of Independence and then again in making the Constitution, to alter or abolish their form of government. The Bill of Rights merely enumerated certain constitutional rights to limit the power of the national government. *It subtracted nothing.* The Ninth Amendment itself creates no new constitutional rights. It is a classic lawyer's "rule of construction" such as one might see near the end of a contract, added in an excess of caution: do not construe the creation of a bill of rights as repealing anything else, or as assigning all rights into the hands of the national government.

The Tenth Amendment likewise explains:

> The powers not delegated to the United States by the Constitution, nor prohibited by it to the States, are reserved to the States respectively, or to the people.

That is, adoption of the Bill of Rights does not change the fact that the national government is one of limited, enumerated powers (even if some powers are written in broad terms). If the national government's actions do not fall within one or another of the Constitution's grants of power, those actions are unconstitutional. The powers not delegated to the national government are reserved to the states. The Tenth Amendment, like the Ninth, is thus a "rule of construction": *do not take the fact that we found it necessary, or prudent, to add a bill of rights as in any way suggesting a change from the idea that the government has only the enumerated powers specifically listed.* The Tenth Amendment forbids Hamilton's warned-of inference that a bill of rights might be taken to enlarge government powers.

The Tenth Amendment is also significant for what it does *not* say. As noted earlier, Madison and the Federalists deliberately chose not to include the word "expressly" before the word "delegated" and fought off all efforts of Anti-Federalists to include such a limitation. As a result, the Tenth Amendment actually serves to reaffirm the Constitution's original plan of enumerated—but broad—powers. The Bill of Rights thus ends its enumeration of rights of the people with a reiteration of the *powers* of the people under the new government, divided between the national government and the governments of the states.

A Second Constitution

The Bill of Rights is an impressive package of freedoms—practically a second Constitution setting forth new checks and balances and limitations on government power. Seen through the rearview mirror of history, moreover, the Bill of Rights can be understood as the completion of the constitutional project begun at Philadelphia in 1787. The adoption of these ten amendments was the final step in the broader process of constitution-making that began with the Constitutional Convention and ended with the ratification of the Bill of Rights by the last of the original states in 1791—just a matter of months after the last state ratified the original Constitution.

The promise of amendments had been critical to getting nine of the thirteen original states to ratify the Constitution. The honoring of that promise—the proposal and adoption of the Bill of Rights—secured the Constitution's adoption by *all* the states of the Union. It is no exaggeration to say that, without the promise of amendments, the Constitution might have been rejected. But the Bill of Rights did more than just help to save the Constitution from its enemies. With the adoption of these amendments, both the Constitution and the Union were more nearly perfected.

But only *more nearly* perfected: even after the addition of the Bill of Rights, the Constitution remained an imperfect, and unproven, framework for government. The Bill of Rights, for all the freedoms it recognized, did not fix everything that was wrong with the original Constitution: slavery, the most fundamental anti-freedom embraced by the Constitution, was left essentially untouched. But the basic freedoms the Bill of Rights *did* protect—freedom of religion, freedom of speech, freedom of the press, and the guarantees of fair trial safeguarding the freedoms of the innocent—would come to play major roles in the nascent United States as the project of government under the new Constitution began to take shape.

Section II

Important Issues for Legal and Criminal Justice

Setting Precedents

Editor's Introduction

This section covers issues of vital importance in the legal and criminal justice field. The first article reviews the exclusionary rule. The historical rationale for the exclusionary rule was to thwart law enforcement's bad faith or outright illegality when it came to search and seizure.

Some issues in the criminal justice world can never be emphasized enough because of their ethical importance and because they illustrate the concept of fundamental fairness to both the government and the defendant. Criminal cases are important to *both* sides. The government represents the interests of crime victims and the populous they serve. The defense represents a defendant charged with a crime.

The first article examines the history and importance of U.S. Supreme Court cases as they pertain to the exclusionary rule. At its most basic, the exclusionary rule excludes evidence seized in a case that was obtained by the government in violation of the defendant's Fourth Amendment right to be free from unreasonable search and seizure. Some of the cases, though handed down decades ago, should inflame the reader with revulsion at the illegal tactics used by law enforcement to obtain evidence. Who can forget Dollree Mapp and the alleged search warrant officers claimed they had before ransacking her home? It bears repeating over and over to students that the citizenry possesses certain fundamental rights.

The second article reviews the road to the suspect's Miranda rights from the 1966 decision *Miranda v. Arizona*, 384 U.S. 436. The history of coerced confessions in this country by law enforcement is highlighted in this article. The *Miranda* decision was applied to the states through the incorporation clause.

The Brady/Giglio disclosure requirements are essential safeguards for a defendant and his or her right to a fair trial. Prosecutors have a duty to the defense to turn over exculpatory evidence. There are cases in every state in this country where prosecutors failed to abide by the law and turn over this evidence. This tactic to hide evidence has resulted in individuals spending years in jail before their convictions were overturned.

The last article, "Is Your Judge for Sale?," illuminates the competing issues when judges run for election. The staggering amounts of money involved in these elections and the tactics used by competitors for the judgeship are showcased and hardly conjure up the image of judges that most people would like to maintain—one of wisdom, decorum, and evenhandedness. This article is a sad commentary on how judgeships are bought by the individual who runs the most slanderous and moneyed campaign.

Reading 2.1

The Exclusionary Rule

Rolando V. del Carmen and Jeffery T. Walker

Introduction

The exclusionary rule provides that any evidence obtained by the government in violation of the Fourth Amendment right against unreasonable searches and seizures is not admissible in a court of law. It is a judge-made rule whose purpose is to deter police misconduct; the assumption being that, if evidence obtained by the police in violation of the Fourth Amendment cannot be used in court, police misconduct will be minimized.

Evidence obtained by the police in violation of other rights under the Bill of Rights (such as the privilege against self-incrimination under the Fifth Amendment, or the right to counsel under the Sixth Amendment) is not admissible in court either, but that exclusion does not come under the exclusionary rule; rather, the evidence is excluded based on a violation of the constitutional right to due process. The exclusionary rule, therefore, is of limited application in that it applies only in cases involving violations of the prohibition against unreasonable searches and seizures under the Fourth Amendment.

The first exclusionary rule case decided by the United States Supreme Court was *Boyd v. United States* (116 U.S. 616) in 1886. In that case, the Court held that the forced disclosure of papers amounting to evidence of a crime violated the Fourth Amendment right of the suspect and, therefore, the evidence could not be used in court. In 1914, in *Weeks v. United States* (32 U.S. 383), the Court held that evidence illegally obtained by federal officers could not be used in federal criminal prosecutions. *Mapp v. Ohio*, 467 U.S. 643 (1961) is the leading and best-known case on the exclusionary rule. In *Mapp*, the Court held that the exclusionary rule also applied to state criminal prosecutions, thus extending the exclusionary rule to all federal and state criminal proceedings.

There are many exceptions to the exclusionary rule, as the cases briefed here show. The common theme in these cases is that the misconduct, mistake, or error was not committed by the police but by other government officials—in some cases judges, the legislature, or a court clerk. The evidence obtained can be used in court because the exclusionary rule was meant to deter police misconduct, not the misconduct of other government officials.

Although originally controversial, the exclusionary rule has been accepted and applied by the courts and is now an accepted part of policing. The United States Supreme Court continues to define exceptions, but the exclusionary rule is here to stay as a form of protection against violations by the police of the public's right against unreasonable searches and seizures.

The leading cases briefed in this chapter on the exclusionary rule are *Mapp v. Ohio* and *Weeks v. United States*.

Weeks v. United States 232 U.S. 383 (1914)

CAPSULE: Evidence illegally seized by federal law enforcement officers is not admissible in a federal criminal prosecution.

FACTS: Weeks was arrested for using the mail to transport tickets for a lottery. Other officers searched Weeks' home without a warrant and seized various articles and papers that were then turned over to the United States Marshals Service. Later in the day, police officers returned with a Marshal and again searched Weeks' home without a warrant and seized letters and other articles. Weeks was charged with and convicted of unlawful use of the mail.

ISSUE: Is evidence illegally obtained by federal law enforcement officers admissible in court? NO.

SUPREME COURT DECISION: Evidence illegally seized by federal law enforcement officers is not admissible in federal criminal prosecutions.

REASON: The Fourth Amendment freedom from unreasonable searches and seizures applies "... to all invasions on the part of the government and its employees of the sanctity of a man's home and the privacies of life. It is not the breaking of his doors and the rummaging of his drawers that constitutes the essence of the offense; but it is the invasion of his indefeasible right of personal security, personal liberty and private property."

CASE SIGNIFICANCE: This decision excluded illegally obtained evidence from use in federal prosecutions. This rule was extended to state criminal prosecutions in 1961 in *Mapp v. Ohio*,

367 U.S. 643 (1961), making illegally obtained evidence inadmissible in both state and federal courts. It is interesting to note that from 1914 to 1960, federal courts admitted evidence of a federal crime if it was obtained illegally by state officers, as long as there was no connivance with federal officers. This questionable practice was known as the "silver platter doctrine." In 1960, the Court rejected the "silver platter doctrine" (*Elkins v. United States*, 364 U.S. 206), holding that the Fourth Amendment prohibited the use of illegally obtained evidence in federal prosecutions whether it was obtained by federal or state officers.

Rochin v. California 342 U.S. 165 (1952)

CAPSULE: Some searches are so "shocking to the conscience" that they require exclusion of the evidence seized based on due process.

FACTS: Having information that Rochin was selling narcotics, police officers entered his home and forced their way into the bedroom. When asked about two capsules lying beside the bed, Rochin put them in his mouth. After an unsuccessful attempt to recover them by force, the officers took Rochin to the hospital where his stomach was pumped. Two capsules containing morphine were recovered. A motion to suppress this evidence was denied and Rochin was convicted in a California state court of possession of morphine.

ISSUE: Were the capsules recovered as a result of pumping Rochin's stomach admissible as evidence in court? NO.

SUPREME COURT DECISION: Although searches by state law enforcement officers are not governed by the exclusionary rule, some searches are so "shocking to the conscience" as to require exclusion of the evidence seized based on the due process (fundamental fairness) clause of the Constitution. These cases are limited to acts of coercion, violence, and brutality.

REASON: "... [T]he proceedings by which this conviction was obtained do more than offend some fastidious squeamishness or private sentimentalism about combating crime too energetically. This is conduct that shocks the conscience. Illegally breaking into the privacy of the petitioner, the struggle to open his mouth and remove what was there, the forcible extraction of his stomach's contents—this course of proceeding by agents of the government to obtain evidence is bound to offend even hardened sensibilities. They are methods too close to the rack and screw to permit of constitutional differentiation."

CASE SIGNIFICANCE: This case was decided prior to the extension of the exclusionary rule to the states in 1961. In this state prosecution, however, the Court decided that the evidence obtained could not be used in court, not because of the exclusionary rule, but because the conduct of the police officers was shocking and therefore violated Rochin's right to due process guaranteed by the Fourteenth Amendment. If the case were to be decided today, the evidence would be excluded under the exclusionary rule, not under the due process clause.

Mapp v. Ohio 367 U.S. 643 (1961)

CAPSULE: The exclusionary rule applies to all state criminal proceedings.

FACTS: Mapp was convicted of possession of lewd and lascivious books, pictures, and photographs in violation of Ohio law. Three Cleveland police officers went to Mapp's residence based on information that a person who was wanted in connection with a recent bombing was hiding out in her home. The officers knocked on the door and demanded entrance, but Mapp, telephoning her attorney, refused to admit them without a warrant. The officers again sought entrance three hours later, after the arrival of more police. When Mapp did not respond, the officers broke the door open. Mapp's attorney arrived but was denied access to his client. Mapp demanded to see the search warrant the police claimed to possess. When a paper supposed to be the warrant was held up by one of the officers, Mapp grabbed the paper and placed it in her bosom. A struggle ensued and the paper was recovered after Mapp was handcuffed for being belligerent. A search of the house produced a trunk that contained obscene materials. The materials were admitted into evidence at the trial and Mapp was convicted of possession of obscene materials.

ISSUE: Is evidence obtained in violation of the Fourth Amendment protection from unreasonable searches and seizures admissible in state criminal prosecutions? NO.

SUPREME COURT DECISION: The exclusionary rule, applicable in federal cases, which prohibits the use of evidence obtained as a result of unreasonable searches and seizures also applies to state criminal proceedings.

REASON: "Since the Fourth Amendment's right of privacy has been declared enforceable against the States through the Due Process Clause of the Fourteenth [Amendment], it is enforceable against them by the same sanction of exclusion as is used against the Federal Government. Were it otherwise, then just as without the Weeks rule the assurance against unreasonable searches and seizures would be 'a form of words,' valueless and undeserving of mention in a perpetual charter of inestimable human liberties, so too, without that rule the freedom from state invasions of privacy would be … ephemeral …"

CASE SIGNIFICANCE: *Mapp* is significant because the Court held that the exclusionary rule was thereafter to be applied to all states, thus forbidding both state and federal courts from accepting evidence obtained in violation of the constitutional protection against unreasonable searches and seizures. In the mind of the Court, the facts in *Mapp* illustrate what can happen if police conduct is not restricted. *Mapp* was therefore an ideal case for the Court to use in settling an issue that had to be addressed: whether the exclusionary rule should apply to state criminal proceedings. The Court answered with a definite yes.

Wong Sun v. United States 371 U.S. 471 (1963)

CAPSULE: Evidence obtained as a result of illegal acts by the police must be excluded. In addition, the "fruit of the poisonous tree" of that illegal act must also be excluded. Evidence that has been purged of the primary taint, however, is admissible.

FACTS: Federal narcotics agents arrested Hom Way and found heroin in his possession. Although Way had not been an informant before, the agents went to "Oye's Laundry" based upon his statement that he had bought the heroin from "Blackie Toy," who owned the laundry. At the laundry, agent Wong got James Wah Toy to open the door by telling him that he was calling for dry cleaning. Upon announcing that he was a federal agent, Toy slammed the door and started running. The agents then broke open the door and began to chase Toy. Toy was placed under arrest in his bedroom. A search of the premises uncovered no drugs. There was nothing to link Toy to "Blackie Toy." Upon interrogation, he stated that he had not been selling narcotics but knew that an individual named Johnny had. He told the officers where Johnny lived, and described the bedroom where the heroin was kept and where he had smoked some of the heroin the night before. Based on this information, the agents went to the home of Johnny Yee and found him in possession of an ounce of heroin. Upon interrogation, Yee stated that he had bought the heroin from Toy and an individual named "Sea Dog." Further questioning of Toy revealed that "Sea Dog's" name was Wong Sun. Toy then took the agents to a multifamily dwelling where Wong Sun lived. After identifying himself, agent Wong was admitted by Wong Sun's wife who said he was in the back, asleep. Wong Sun was arrested by the agents. A search pursuant to the arrest found no narcotics. Each of the offenders was arraigned and released on his own recognizance. A few days later, Toy, Yee, and Wong Sun were interrogated again and written statements were made.

Neither Toy nor Wong Sun signed their statements, but Wong Sun admitted to the accuracy of his statement. At the trial, the government's evidence consisted of: (1) the statements made by Toy at the time of his arrest; (2) the heroin taken from Yee; (3) Toy's pretrial statement; and (4) Wong Sun's pretrial statement. Wong Sun and Toy were convicted of transportation and concealment of heroin.

ISSUES: There were a number of issues in this case, but the important issues related to the exclusionary rule are:

1. Were the statements made by Toy after an unlawful arrest admissible? NO.
2. Were the narcotics taken from Yee after an unlawful arrest admissible? NO.
3. Was Wong Sun's statement admissible? YES.

SUPREME COURT DECISION: Statements or evidence obtained indirectly as a result of an unlawful arrest or search are not admissible in court because they are "tainted fruit of the poisonous tree." A suspect's intervening act of free will, however, breaks the chain of illegality, purges the evidence of the taint, and makes the evidence admissible.

REASON: The exclusionary rule has traditionally barred from trial physical, tangible materials obtained either during or as a direct result of an unlawful invasion. "... Thus, verbal evidence which derives so immediately from an unlawful entry and an unauthorized arrest as the officers' action in the present case is no less the 'fruit' of official illegality than the more common tangible fruits of the unwarranted intrusion ..."

"We turn now to the case of ... Wong Sun. We have no occasion to disagree with the finding of the Court of Appeals that his arrest, also, was without probable cause or reasonable grounds. For Wong Sun's unsigned confession was not the fruit of that arrest, and was therefore properly admitted at trial. On the evidence that Wong Sun had been released on his own recognizance after a lawful arraignment, and had returned voluntarily several days later to make the statement, we hold that the connection between the arrest and the statement had 'become so attenuated as to dissipate the taint.'"

CASE SIGNIFICANCE: This case addresses the "tainted fruit of the poisonous tree" aspect of the exclusionary rule. The exclusionary rule provides that evidence obtained in violation of the Fourth Amendment prohibition against unreasonable searches and seizures is not admissible in a court of law. The rule goes beyond that, however, and also says that any other evidence obtained directly or indirectly as a result of the illegal behavior is not admissible either. Hence, once an illegal act has been proved, any evidence obtained either directly or indirectly cannot be admitted in court either under the concept of the original illegality or as the "tainted fruit."

This case also carves out an exception to the exclusionary rule: the "purged taint" exception. What it says is that, despite the initial illegality, the evidence may nonetheless be admissible if it has been purged of the initial taint. An example is this case, in which the statement of Wong Sun, which initially was the product of unlawful behavior by the agents, was nonetheless admitted because of subsequent events. What happened was that after Wong Sun was released on his own recognizance and after lawful arraignment, he returned several days later and made a statement that was then admitted by the trial court. The Court said that the voluntary return by Wong Sun purged the evidence of the initial taint and therefore made the statement admissible.

Nix v. Williams 467 U.S. 431 (1984)

CAPSULE: Illegally obtained evidence may be admissible if the police can prove that they would have discovered the evidence anyway through lawful means.

FACTS: On December 24, a 10-year-old girl disappeared from a YMCA building in Des Moines, Iowa. A short time later, Williams was seen leaving the YMCA with a large bundle wrapped in a blanket. A 14-year-old boy who helped him carry the bundle reported that he had seen "two legs in it and they were skinny and white." William's car was found the next day, 160 miles east of Des Moines. Items of clothing belonging to the missing child and a blanket like the one used to wrap the bundle were found at a rest stop between the YMCA in Des Moines and where the car was found. Assuming that the girl's body could be found between the YMCA and the car, a massive search was conducted. Meanwhile, Williams was arrested by police in a town near where the car was found and was arraigned. Williams' counsel was informed that Williams would be returned to Des Moines without being interrogated. During the trip, an officer began a conversation with Williams in which he said the girl should be given a Christian burial before a snowstorm which might prevent the body from being found. As Williams and the officer neared the town where the body was hidden, Williams agreed to take the officer to the child's body. The body was found about two miles from one of the search teams. At the trial, a motion to suppress the evidence was denied and Williams was convicted of first degree murder. Williams sought release on habeas corpus in U.S. District Court. That court ruled that the evidence had been wrongly admitted at Williams' trial. At his second trial, the prosecutor did not offer Williams' statements into evidence and did not seek to show that Williams had led the police to the body. The trial court ruled that the state had proved that, even if Williams had not led the police to the body, it would have been found by the searchers anyway. Williams was again convicted of murder.

ISSUE: Was the evidence (the body) admissible in court on the theory that the body would ultimately have been discovered anyway because of the ongoing search? YES.

SUPREME COURT DECISION: Evidence that is obtained illegally may be admissible if the police can prove that they would have discovered the evidence anyway through lawful means.

REASON: "The independent source doctrine teaches us that the interest of society in deterring unlawful police conduct and the public interest in having juries receive all probative evidence of a crime are properly balanced by putting the police in the same, not a worse, position than they would have been in if no police error or misconduct had occurred."

CASE SIGNIFICANCE: This case illustrates the "inevitable discovery exception to the exclusionary rule. "Fruit of the poisonous tree" is evidence obtained indirectly as a result of illegal police behavior (such as the illegal discovery of a map that tells where contraband is hidden). This evidence is usually inadmissible due to the illegality of police actions. The exception set out in this case states that evidence that is the "fruit of the poisonous tree" is admissible if the police can prove that they would inevitably have discovered the evidence anyway by lawful means. In this case, no *Miranda* warnings were given to the suspect before he confessed; hence, the evidence obtained was excluded during the first trial. But because the evidence would have been discovered anyway as a result of the continued search, the Court said that the evidence could be admitted.

United States v. Leon 468 U.S. 897 (1984)

CAPSULE: The exclusionary rule allows the use of evidence obtained by officers who are acting in reasonable reliance on a search warrant that is later declared invalid.

FACTS: Acting on the basis of information from a confidential informant, officers initiated a drug trafficking investigation. Based on an affidavit summarizing the police officer's observation, a search warrant was prepared. The warrant was reviewed by three Deputy District Attorneys and issued by a state court judge. Ensuing searches produced large quantities of drugs. Leon was indicted on drug charges. Motions to suppress the evidence were granted in part because the affidavit was insufficient to establish probable cause. The court rejected the notion of good faith of the officer and acquitted the defendants.

ISSUE: Is evidence obtained as the result of a search conducted pursuant to a warrant that was issued by a neutral and detached magistrate admissible in court if the warrant is ultimately found invalid through no fault of the police officer? YES.

SUPREME COURT DECISION: The Fourth Amendment's exclusionary rule allows the use of evidence obtained by officers acting in reasonable reliance on a search warrant issued by a neutral and detached magistrate that is ultimately found invalid.

REASON: "In the ordinary case, an officer cannot be expected to question the magistrate's probable cause determination or his judgment that the form of the warrant is technically sufficient. '[O]nce the warrant issues, there is literally nothing more the policeman can do in seeking to comply with the law.' Penalizing the officer for the magistrate's error, rather than his own, cannot logically contribute to the deterrence of Fourth Amendment violations."

CASE SIGNIFICANCE: This case, together with *Massachusetts v. Sheppard*, 468 U.S. 981 (1984), which was decided on the same day, are arguably the most important cases decided on the exclusionary rule since *Mapp v. Ohio*, 367 U.S. 643 (1961). They represent a significant, although narrow, exception to that doctrine. In these two cases, the Court said that there were objectively reasonable grounds for the officers' mistaken belief that the warrants authorized the searches. The officers took every step that could reasonably have been taken to ensure that the warrants were valid. The difference between the *Leon* and *Sheppard* cases is that, in *Sheppard*, the issue was improper use of a search warrant form (the form used was used in another district to search for controlled substances, the judge telling the detective who filed the form that the necessary changes would be made by the judge), whereas in *Leon* the issue was the use of a questionable informant and stale information. The cases are similar, however, in that the mistakes were made by the judges, not the police. The Court said that the evidence in both cases was admissible because the judge, not the police, erred and the exclusionary rule is designed to control the conduct of the police, not the conduct of judges.

Massachusetts v. Sheppard 468 U.S. 981 (1984)

CAPSULE: Evidence obtained as a result of a search in which the police acted in reliance on a search warrant that was subsequently declared invalid by the court is admissible as an exception to the exclusionary rule.

FACTS: Based on evidence gathered in a homicide investigation, a police officer drafted an affidavit to support an application for a search warrant and an arrest warrant. The affidavit was reviewed and approved by the District Attorney. Because it was Sunday, the officer had difficulty finding a warrant application form. The officer ultimately found a used search warrant authorizing a search for controlled substances. After making some changes, the officer presented the warrant to a judge at his residence. The judge was informed that the warrant might need further changes. Concluding that the affidavit established probable cause for the search, the judge made some corrections and signed the warrant. He then returned the warrant to the officer with the assurance that it was sufficient authority to carry out the search. The ensuing search was limited to the items listed in the affidavit. Several pieces of incriminating evidence were found and Sheppard was arrested. At a pretrial motion to suppress, the judge ruled that the warrant was invalid, but the evidence was admitted based on the officer's good faith in executing what he believed to be a valid warrant. Sheppard was convicted of first degree murder.

ISSUE: Is evidence that is obtained from a search that is based on a warrant that is later declared invalid because of error by the issuing magistrate admissible in court? YES.

SUPREME COURT DECISION: Evidence obtained by the police acting in good faith, based on a search warrant that was issued by a neutral and detached magistrate, but that was later found to be invalid, is admissible in court as an exception to the exclusionary rule.

REASON: "Having already decided [in Leon] that the exclusionary rule should not be applied when the officer conducting the search acted in objectively reasonable reliance on a warrant issued by a detached and neutral magistrate that subsequently is determined to be invalid, the sole issue before us in this case is whether the officers reasonably believed that the search they conducted was authorized by a valid warrant. There is no dispute that the officers believed that the warrant authorized the search that they conducted. Thus, the only question is whether there was an objectively reasonable basis for the officers' mistaken belief. ... The officers in this case took every step that could reasonably be expected of them. ... [A] reasonable officer would have concluded, as O'Malley did, that the warrant authorized a search for the materials outlined in the affidavit. ... Sheppard contends that since O'Malley knew the warrant form was defective, he should have examined it to make sure that the necessary changes had been made. However, that argument is based on the premise that O'Malley had a duty to disregard the judge's assurances that the requested search would be authorized and the necessary changes would be made. ... [W]e refuse to rule that an officer is required to disbelieve a judge who has just advised him, by word and by action, that the warrant he possesses authorizes him to conduct the search he has requested."

CASE SIGNIFICANCE: As indicated in the *Leon* case, above, *Sheppard* was the second case involving the exclusionary rule decided by the Court on the same day. These cases dealt with incidents in which mistakes were made, not by the police, but by the magistrates who issued the warrants. Both cases carved out a significant exception to the exclusionary rule: that evidence is admissible if the mistake was made by a magistrate rather than by the police. Note, however, that this is a very narrow "good faith" exception. The police acted "in good faith" in these cases; but it cannot be said that evidence is admissible every time the police act "in good faith." For example, if the police acted illegally in obtaining evidence, they cannot later claim to have acted in good faith in arguing for the admissibility of the evidence obtained, even if they actually did act in good faith and can prove it. This is because the error was committed by the police, not a third person. In the *Sheppard* case, the error was committed by the magistrate, not the police. This is an important difference.

Murray v. United States 487 U.S. 533 (1988)

CAPSULE: The exclusionary rule allows the use of evidence obtained by officers who act in reasonable reliance on a search warrant that is later declared invalid.

FACTS: Suspecting illegal drug activities, federal agents followed Murray and several co-conspirators. At one point, Murray drove a truck and another person drove a camper into a warehouse. Twenty minutes later, when the two emerged from the warehouse, law enforcement agents could see a tractor-trailer bearing a long, dark container. The truck and camper were later turned over to other drivers who were arrested and found in possession of marijuana.

Upon receiving this information, the law enforcement agents returned to the warehouse, without a warrant, and forced entry. The warehouse was unoccupied but the agents observed, in plain view, several burlap-wrapped bales of marijuana. The law enforcement agents left the warehouse without disturbing the bales and did not reenter until they had a valid search warrant. In applying for the warrant, the agents did not mention the forced entry into the warehouse and did not rely on any information obtained during that search. After obtaining the warrant, law enforcement agents returned to the warehouse and seized numerous bales of marijuana and a notebook listing the destinations of the bales. Murray was arrested and convicted of conspiracy to possess and distribute illegal drugs.

ISSUE: Is evidence first observed in an illegal entry by officers but subsequently seized through a valid, independent, search warrant admissible in court? YES.

SUPREME COURT DECISION: Even if the police illegally enter private property, evidence initially discovered during that illegal entry may be admissible in court if it is later discovered during a valid search that is wholly unrelated to the illegal entry.

REASON: The Court reasoned that the evidence ought not to have been excluded just because of unrelated illegal conduct by the police. If probable cause for a search warrant can be established apart from any illegal activity by the police, the evidence obtained in the subsequent search should be admissible.

CASE SIGNIFICANCE: This case illustrates the "independent source" exception to the exclusionary rule. In this case, the police illegally entered the warehouse and discovered bales of marijuana. The Court said that the marijuana would be admissible if the officers later searched the warehouse pursuant to a valid warrant that was issued based on information that was not obtained during the illegal entry. An initial illegal entry, therefore, does not automatically exclude the evidence if the evidence is not seized at the time of the illegal entry, but pursuant to a valid warrant that is later obtained without relying on information obtained during the illegal entry.

Minnesota v. Olson 495 U.S. 91 (1989)

CAPSULE: Warrantless nonconsensual entry of a residence by police to arrest an overnight guest violates the Fourth Amendment.

FACTS: The police suspected Olson of being the driver of the getaway car involved in a robbery-murder. Based on an anonymous tip, the police surrounded the home of two women with whom they believed Olson had been staying as a guest. A detective then telephoned the home and told one of the women that Olson should come outside, whereupon he heard a male voice saying, "Tell them I left." When the woman told the detective this, he ordered the police to enter. Without permission or a search warrant, and with their weapons drawn, the police entered the house and arrested Olson, who was hiding in a closet. Based on an incriminating statement made by Olson, he was convicted of murder, armed robbery, and assault.

ISSUE: Is the Fourth Amendment violated when the police make a warrantless, nonconsensual entry and arrest without exigent (emergency) circumstances? YES.

SUPREME COURT DECISION: The warrantless non-consensual entry by the police of a residence to arrest an overnight guest violates the Fourth Amendment, unless justified by exigent circumstances.

REASON: "... [W]e think that society recognizes that a houseguest has a legitimate expectation of privacy in his host's home." An overnight guest "... seeks shelter in another's home precisely because it provides him with privacy, a place where he and his possessions will not be disturbed by anyone except his host and those his host allows inside. ... The houseguest is there with the permission of his host, who is willing to share his house and his privacy with the guest. ... The host may admit or exclude from the house as he prefers, but it is unlikely that he will admit someone who wants to see or meet with the guest over the objection of the guest." Hosts, therefore, "... will more likely than not respect the privacy interests of their guests, who are entitled to a legitimate expectation of privacy despite the fact that they have no legal interest in the premises and do not have the legal authority to determine who may or may not enter the household." Because Olson's "... expectation of privacy in the host's home was rooted in 'understandings that are recognized and permitted by society,' it was legitimate, and respondent can claim the protection of the Fourth Amendment."

CASE SIGNIFICANCE: This case establishes the principle that the arrest of a suspect in another person's home requires a warrant for entry into the home, except: (1) if exigent circumstances are present, or (2) if consent is given by the owner of the house. In this case, suspect Olson was an overnight guest in the home. There was no reason to believe that he would flee the premises, hence exigent circumstances were not deemed present. The Court ruled that the police should have obtained a search warrant to enable them to enter the house legally. An overnight guest has an expectation of privacy that society is prepared to recognize as reasonable, hence a warrant should have been obtained. The statement made after his arrest was not admissible in court.

Arizona v. Evans 514 U.S. 1 (1995)

CAPSULE: The exclusionary rule does not require suppression of evidence seized in violation of the Fourth Amendment where the erroneous information resulted from clerical errors of court employees.

FACTS: Police officers saw Evans going the wrong way on a one-way street in front of the police station. When Evans was stopped, officers determined that his driver's license had been suspended. When Evans' name was entered into a computer data terminal in the officer's patrol car, it indicated that there was an outstanding misdemeanor warrant for Evans' arrest. While being handcuffed, Evans dropped a hand-rolled cigarette that turned out to be marijuana. A search of Evans' car revealed more marijuana under the passenger's seat. At trial, Evans moved to suppress the evidence as fruit of an unlawful arrest because the arrest warrant for the misdemeanor had been quashed 17 days prior to his arrest but was not entered into the computer due to a clerical error of a court employee. Evans also argued that the good faith exception to the exclusionary rule was inapplicable in this case. These motions were denied and Evans was convicted.

ISSUE: Does the exclusionary rule require suppression of evidence that is seized by an officer acting in reliance on erroneous information resulting from clerical errors of court employees? NO.

SUPREME COURT DECISION: "The exclusionary rule does not require suppression of evidence seized in violation of the Fourth Amendment where the erroneous information resulted from clerical errors of court employees."

REASON: "The exclusionary rule operates as a judicially created remedy designed to safeguard against future violations [by police officers] of Fourth Amendment rights through the rule's deterrent effect." The application of the exclusionary rule was for police officers rather than court employees (see *United States v. Leon*, 468 U.S. 897 [1974]). The Court found "... no sound reason to apply the exclusionary rule as a means of deterring misconduct on the part of judicial officers" because application of the exclusionary rule to court personnel could not be expected to alter the behavior of the arresting officer. Furthermore "[t]here [was] no indication that the arresting officer was not acting objectively reasonably when he relied upon the police computer record. Application of the *Leon* framework supports a categorical exception to the exclusionary rule for clerical errors of court employees."

CASE SIGNIFICANCE: This case extends an exception to the exclusionary rule when an error is committed by court employees rather than the police. The exclusionary rule was fashioned to deter police misconduct, hence the Court refused to apply it to cases in which the error was not made by the police. Previous cases have held that if the error is made by a magistrate (as in *Massachusetts v. Sheppard* and *United States v. Leon*), or by the legislature (as in *Illinois v. Krull*), the exclusionary rule does not apply. The theme in these cases is that if the error is not committed by the police, then the exclusionary rule should not apply because it was meant to control the behavior of the police. Evans, therefore, is consistent with the

Court's holdings in previous cases and came as no surprise. The unanswered question is whether error by any public officer other than the police would be an addition to this rule. The dissent in *Evans* argued that the Fourth Amendment prohibition against unreasonable searches and seizures applies to the conduct of all government officers, not just the police. The majority in *Evans* disagreed, preferring instead to focus on the original purpose of the exclusionary rule—which is to control police conduct.

Brigham City, Utah v. Stuart et al. 547 U.S. 47 (2006)

CAPSULE: "Police may enter a home without a warrant when they have an objectively reasonable basis for believing that an occupant is seriously injured or imminently threatened with such injury."

FACTS: Officers responded to a call regarding a loud party at a residence. Upon arriving at the house, they heard shouting from inside. They also observed two juveniles drinking beer in the backyard. They entered the backyard and saw through a screen door and windows a fight taking place in the kitchen of the home involving four adults and a juvenile. After observing several people being punched, the officers then opened the screen door and announced their presence with no response from the occupants. The officers entered the kitchen and again announced their presence, at which time the fight then ceased. The officers arrested the adults and charged them with contributing to the delinquency of a minor, disorderly conduct, and intoxication.

ISSUE: May the police enter a home without a warrant when they have an objectively reasonable belief that an occupant is seriously injured or imminently threatened with injury? Yes.

SUPREME COURT DECISION: "Police may enter a home without a warrant when they have an objectively reasonable basis for believing that an occupant is seriously injured or imminently threatened with such injury."

REASON: "It is a 'basic principle of Fourth Amendment law that searches and seizures inside a home without a warrant are presumptively unreasonable.'" [internal citations omitted]. "One exigency obviating the requirement of a warrant is the need to assist persons who are seriously injured or threatened with such injury." "Accordingly, law enforcement officers may enter a home without a warrant to render emergency assistance to an injured occupant or to protect an occupant from imminent injury."

CASE SIGNIFICANCE: In this case, the Court ruled that police may justifiably enter a home or building without a warrant if they have an "objectively reasonable" basis (lower than probable cause) to believe that somebody inside is "seriously injured or threatened with such injury." The Court added that "the need to protect or preserve life or avoid serious injury is justification for what would be otherwise illegal absent an exigency or emergency." This reiterates the "danger to third person" or "emergency aid" exception to the warrant requirement. The other notable instances when the police may enter a building or home without a warrant are: (1) when there is danger of physical harm to the officer or destruction of evidence, and (2) in cases of "hot pursuit." All three exceptions may be classified under "exigent circumstances."

Davis v. Washington 547 U.S. 813 (2006)

CAPSULE: "Statements are nontestimonial [and therefore admissible in court] when made in the course of police interrogation under circumstances objectively indicating that the primary purpose of interrogation is to enable police assistance to meet an ongoing emergency."

FACTS: After a call and hang-up to 911, the operator reversed the call and Michelle McCottry answered. Based on questioning McCottry, the operator determined she was involved in a domestic disturbance with her former boyfriend, Davis. The operator learned that Davis had just left in a car with another person after hitting McCottry. Officers arrived and observed the injuries to McCottry but had no way to determine the cause of the injuries. Davis was later charged with violating a domestic no-contact order. Over Davis's objection, the 911 tape was admitted into evidence and he was convicted. Davis appealed his conviction, saying that his constitutional right to cross-examination was violated by the admission of the tape-recording into evidence because there was no opportunity to cross-examine.

ISSUE: Are statements made to law enforcement personnel during a 911 call or at a crime scene "testimonial" and thus subject to the requirements of the Sixth Amendment's right to cross-examination and confrontation? No.

SUPREME COURT DECISION: "Statements are nontestimonial [and therefore admissible in court] when made in the course of police interrogation under circumstances objectively indicating that the primary purpose of interrogation is to enable police assistance to meet an ongoing emergency."

REASON: "The Confrontation Clause of the Sixth Amendment provides: 'In all criminal prosecutions, the accused shall enjoy the right ... to be confronted with the witnesses against him.' In *Crawford* v. *Washington*, 541 U.S. 36, 53–54 (2004), we held that this provision bars 'admission of testimonial statements of a witness who did not appear at trial unless he was unavailable to testify, and the defendant had had a prior opportunity for cross-examination.' A critical portion of this holding, and the portion central to resolution of the two cases now before us, is the phrase 'testimonial statements.' Only statements of this sort cause the declarant to be a 'witness' within the meaning of the Confrontation Clause. See *id.*, at 51. It is the testimonial character of the statement that separates it from other hearsay that, while subject to traditional limitations upon hearsay evidence, is not subject to the Confrontation Clause." "A 911 call ... and at least the initial interrogation conducted in connection with a 911 call, is ordinarily not designed primarily to 'establis[h] or prov[e]' some past fact, but to describe current circumstances requiring police assistance." "We conclude from all this that the circumstances of McCottry's interrogation objectively indicate its primary purpose was to enable police assistance to meet an ongoing emergency. She simply was not acting as a *witness*; she was not *testifying*." [emphasis in original].

CASE SIGNIFICANCE: This is an important case in police work because it holds that tape-recordings of calls to the police may be admissible in court during trial as evidence as long as they are non-testimonial. Every day the police, through the 911 service, receive all kinds of calls that are recorded, including those that may be incriminating to the accused, such as in this case. Davis claimed that admitting the recording violated his right to cross-examination because the taped evidence could not be cross-examined. The Court rejected that claim, ruling that for purposes of admissibility as evidence in court, a distinction should be made between non-testimonial and testimonial evidence. Non-testimonial statements recorded through 911 are admissible, whereas testimonial statements are not. The Court then gave this distinction: "Statements are non-testimonial when made in the course of police interrogation under circumstances objectively indicating that the primary purpose of interrogation is to enable police assistance to meet an ongoing emergency." By contrast, the Court stated that statements "are testimonial when the circumstances objectively indicate that there is no such ongoing emergency, and that the primary purpose of the interrogation is to establish or prove past events relevant to later criminal prosecution." This distinction gives general guidance to police and prosecution as to what statements are admissible and what are not.

The Road to Miranda

Scott D. Seligman

I N ITS RULING IN THE CASE of *Ziang Sung Wan v. United States*, the Supreme Court had broken new ground in American criminal justice, reaffirming the principle first stated in *Bram v. United States* that the Fifth Amendment permitted only voluntary confessions to be admitted as evidence in federal proceedings. It had also stated explicitly that excluding only those made in response to promises or threats was simply too narrow a test for voluntariness.

But two additional, important challenges lay ahead before all of America's accused could enjoy full protection under this new principle of law. First, the new standard applied only to cases before the federal courts, where the Constitution indisputably governed. The privileges promised the accused in the Bill of Rights had not yet been determined to apply to the states and localities. This convoluted process, known as the "incorporation doctrine," actually took decades. In *Lawlessness in Law Enforcement*, the Wickersham Commission had pointed out countless examples of coerced confessions on the state and local levels, but it had not specifically discussed, in its paltry list of recommendations, the need to extend the standard articulated in *Wan* beyond the federal system. Many state courts nonetheless took immediate note of the *Wan* decision and cited it to support their use of the voluntariness standard.

Second, the new standard lacked clarity. For all the elegance of its *Wan* decision, the Taft court hadn't really replaced the old test with anything tangible. Brandeis hadn't provided a satisfactory definition of "voluntariness" or instructions on how to ensure it. He had found that "a confession obtained by compulsion must be excluded whatever may have been the character of the compulsion" but he had made no attempt to delimit the ingredients of "compulsion." As a result the concept remained open to interpretation and the standard was inconsistently applied. For all his eloquence, the good justice had left the country with a shining principle that was something of a tautology. As a result, abuses unfortunately continued.

If state judiciaries were to be held to the *Wan* standard, the stage would first have to be set. The Supreme Court would need to step in again, more than once. It opened the door in 1932 in the case of *Powell v. Alabama*. This was the famous case of the "Scottsboro Boys," nine southern black teenagers who had been accused of raping a white woman. The young men, all but one of whom were convicted and sentenced to death in rushed trials that lasted just a day, had been given no advance access to attorneys, nor had they even been told before their trials that they had a right to counsel.

After the Alabama Supreme Court upheld all but one of their convictions, the defendants appealed to the U.S. Supreme Court. In a 7–2 decision, the court ordered new trials, ruling that the "due process clause" of the Fourteenth Amendment—the stipulation that "no person shall be deprived of life, liberty of property without due process of law"—had been violated.[1]

Powell v. Alabama had nothing to do with confessions. It was about fairness and the right to counsel, enshrined in the Sixth Amendment, not the Fifth. But the court decided that it was one of the fundamental rights guaranteed to all by the Constitution and that state courts were every bit as bound to respect it as federal courts. The case was thus a watershed: the ruling marked the first time the Supreme Court had reversed a *state-level* criminal conviction on *constitutional* grounds. It did not guarantee Fifth Amendment rights to state-level defendants but it did find that they were entitled to at least some of the protections of the Sixth Amendment.

It was a beginning.

Four years after *Powell*, another case—also involving black defendants, who were in far more peril than whites of having their rights trampled by the state courts, especially in the Deep South—reached the Supreme Court. *Brown v. Mississippi* was a murder case. Three black tenant farmers accused of killing a white planter had been brutally whipped and one had actually been strung up on a tree, to get them to confess. Their confessions were admitted anyway; as in Wan's case, jurors were simply instructed to weigh them like any other evidence. Despite a total lack of corroborating evidence, the all-white jury had convicted the defendants and sentenced them to death; the Mississippi Supreme Court affirmed the verdicts.

Although the state of Mississippi argued that the U.S. Supreme Court lacked jurisdiction because criminal procedure was under the purview of the states, the justices could hardly ignore the deplorable treatment endured by the *Brown* defendants. Chief Justice Charles Evans Hughes expressed the horror of his colleagues when he observed in his opinion that "the transcript reads more like pages torn from some medieval account than a record made within the confines of a modern civilization." He continued, "It would be difficult to conceive of methods more revolting to the sense of justice than those taken to procure the confessions of these petitioners, and the use of the confessions thus obtained as the basis for conviction and sentence was a clear denial of due process."[2]

But the court did not refer to the voluntariness test in framing the question posed by the case. Its unanimous decision to overturn the convictions of the *Brown* defendants made no mention of the *Wan* case or the Fifth Amendment. Hughes stated the issue as "whether convictions which rest solely upon confessions shown to have been extorted by officers of the State by brutality and violence are consistent with the due process of law required by the Fourteenth Amendment." The upshot was that the standard governing confessions admitted in state courts would henceforth, for all practical purposes, be the same as that of the federal courts.[3]

The Supreme Court continued to hear case after case in which law enforcement ran roughshod over individual rights due to the lack of specificity in that standard. *Brown* had sent a strong signal to the states but in no way had it ended coerced confessions. If anything, the introduction of the due process test, which attempted to assess the fairness of the process through which the confession was obtained, actually muddied the waters even more. Assessing police behavior and its effects on a diverse collection of defendants more or less required a case-by-case analysis. Nor did the due process test supplant the voluntariness principle. In the dozens of cases heard in the three decades following *Brown v. Mississippi* that involved the admissibility of confessions, the court vacillated between assessing voluntariness and fairness.[4]

In *Ashcraft v. Tennessee*, for example, heard in 1944, the court invoked the voluntariness test. The case involved the murder conviction of a man whose confession was elicited through continuous relay interrogations over a thirty-six-hour period. The detectives and prosecutors took time off to sleep but the defendant was denied any rest. Instead of throwing the confession out, however, the judge had put the question of its voluntariness to a jury. The story was eerily reminiscent of Ziang Sung Wan's treatment by the Washington DC police and the trial court. The 1944 Supreme Court found that the circumstances of the man's interrogation were inherently coercive and reversed the verdict, although three justices dissented.[5]

Nearly two decades later, in *Haynes v. Washington* and *Culombe v. Connecticut*, the court looked to the due process standard. In the former, it overruled the State of Washington Supreme Court, which had sustained the verdict against a man found guilty of robbing a gas station. He had been convicted on the strength of a confession wrung from him after police refused his request for an attorney and denied him all contact with the outside world for several days. In the latter case, a thirty-six-year-old "mental defective of the moron class" was held without counsel and questioned intermittently for more than four days, even though he had requested a lawyer; he was later found guilty of murder. As in *Ashcraft*, the voluntariness of the confessions was left to juries to decide, but the court determined that their admission into evidence violated the defendants' due process rights.[6]

The court's frustration and weariness are evident from Justice Felix Frankfurter's opinion in *Culombe*:

> Once again the Court is confronted with the painful duty of sitting in judgment on a State's conviction for murder, after a jury's verdict was found flawless by the State's highest court, in order to determine whether the defendant's confessions, decisive for the conviction, were admitted into evidence in accordance with the standards for admissibility demanded by the Due Process Clause of the Fourteenth Amendment. This recurring problem touching the administration of criminal justice by the States presents in an aggravated form in this case the anxious task of reconciling the responsibility of the police for ferreting out crime with the right of the criminal defendant, however guilty, to be tried according to constitutional requirements.[7]

It was not until 1964 that the court finally got around to stating *explicitly* that the states were bound to uphold the Fifth Amendment's guarantee against self-incrimination. In *Malloy v. Hogan*, a case that had nothing to do with confessions per se, a Connecticut man, on probation after serving three months in jail for illegal gambling, refused to testify in a state inquiry into criminal activities because doing so might have incriminated him. He was found in contempt of court and sent to prison until he agreed to do so. His petition for a writ of habeas corpus was denied; the rejection was upheld on appeal. In a 5–4 opinion that characterized the American legal system as "accusatorial, not inquisitorial," the court held that states were obliged to honor the Fifth Amendment's protection against self-incrimination in their criminal proceedings.[8]

The muddle created by these disparate approaches and the lack of a bright-line test for police, prosecutors, and judges virtually guaranteed that the lower courts could continue to find ways of admitting the confessions of defendants mistreated between arrest and trial. It became palpably clear that voluntariness required more definition; in order to ensure it, police behavior would again have to be explicitly addressed. But this time the remedy would not involve outlawing nefarious police practices that might *negate* voluntariness so much as mandating constructive behavior that would serve to *ensure* it.[9]

For much of the 1950s and nearly all of the following decade, the Supreme Court was under the leadership of Earl Warren, a Republican progressive who served nearly three terms as governor of California before assuming the position of chief justice. The Warren court, made up largely of New Deal liberals appointed by Democratic presidents, was notable for its broad, groundbreaking rulings and its willingness to reexamine and reaffirm the rights of defendants in state and local prosecutions. Warren himself turned out to be far

FIGURE 2.2.1   Chief Justice of the Supreme Court Earl Warren, author of the *Miranda v. Arizona* decision.
Source: Harvard Law School Library.

more liberal than anyone had expected when he was appointed. It was a far cry from the Taft court. The Warren court's many landmark decisions expanded civil rights, civil liberties, and federal power in myriad ways.

In 1966, the court granted petitions for writs of certiorari in four more cases of incommunicado interrogation. In each, a defendant in police custody had been cut off from the outside world and questioned without being informed of his rights. Like Ziang Sung Wan, all four defendants had made incriminating statements that were used to convict them. The cases were handpicked and consolidated because they offered an opportunity for the court to spell out procedures for assuring that individuals were accorded their Fifth Amendment rights against self-incrimination. Chief Justice Warren, who wrote the opinion for the majority, asserted that the cases raised questions that "go to the roots of our concepts of American criminal jurisprudence: the restraints society must observe consistent with the Federal Constitution in prosecuting individuals for crime."[10]

The opinions of the Warren court in the four cases were subsumed under one landmark decision, named for the one listed first on the docket: *Miranda v. Arizona*. In the *Miranda* case, a signed confession was used to convict Ernesto Miranda, a man accused of kidnapping and rape who had had no attorney and had not been advised of his right to counsel.

More than four decades after the *Wan* case, and a quarter-century after Brandeis's death, the learned justice's words were central to the court's reasoning. In his opinion, in which he was joined by four other justices, Chief Justice Warren traced the evolution of the privilege against self-incrimination, noting its ancient roots and its search for "the proper scope of governmental power over the citizen." He remarked that the constitutional foundation underlying the privilege "is the respect a government—state or federal—must accord to the dignity and integrity of its citizens."

He traced the principle through the *Bram* case, in which protection against self-incrimination had been found in the Fifth Amendment, and ultimately the *Wan* case, in which it had finally been divorced from specific police misconduct, distilled, and allowed to stand on its own. He quoted the very same excerpt from Brandeis's opinion that the Wickersham Commission had selected so many years earlier:

> In the Federal courts the requisite of voluntariness is not satisfied by establishing merely that the confession was not induced by a promise or a threat. A confession is voluntary in law if, and only if, it was, in fact, voluntarily made. A confession may have been given voluntarily, although it was made to police officers, while in custody, and in answer to an examination conducted by them. But a confession obtained by compulsion must be excluded, whatever may have been the character of the compulsion and whether the compulsion was applied in a judicial proceeding or otherwise.

The chief justice noted that "the current practice of incommunicado interrogation is at odds with one of our Nation's most cherished principles—that the individual may not be compelled to incriminate himself. Unless adequate protective devices are employed to dispel the compulsion inherent in custodial surroundings, no statement obtained from the defendant can truly be the product of his free choice."

He went on to spell out those safeguards, which were ultimately condensed into the summary statement familiar to most Americans today as "Miranda rights." Warren did not make them up out of whole cloth; he reviewed standard procedures of the Federal Bureau of Investigation—the name given the former Bureau of Investigation in 1935—and consulted police training manuals to determine their best practices. They serve to inform suspects in clear and unequivocal terms that they have a right to remain silent, that anything they say might be used against them in a court of law, that they have the right to counsel, and that, if they are unable to afford one, an attorney will be appointed for them.[11]

Ironically, the issue had come full circle from 1884's *Hopt v. Utah*, which had also concerned itself with police conduct. The difference was that *Hopt* was all about what the police should *not* do in order to ensure voluntary confessions; *Miranda* was about what they *had* to do.

The principle articulated so succinctly and elegantly in *Ziang Sung Wan v. United States* was at the heart of the *Miranda* decision, which finally blended the voluntariness and fairness standards. All the new requirements imposed on law enforcement were ordained in the service of ensuring that only a voluntary confession might ever be used against a defendant in a court of law.

Wan's tribulations had cost him years of freedom but in part because of them Americans would henceforth be protected from the kind of abusive treatment he had received at the hands of the Washington police nearly half a century earlier. The continued relevance of his story is demonstrated in the fact that his case has been cited in ninety federal and seventy-seven state cases in the ninety-plus years since it was decided.

Ziang Sung Wan was still living when the Supreme Court issued its opinion in *Miranda v. Arizona*. He never knew of the case, still less his own role in shaping the decision. Had he been entitled to *Miranda*'s protections in 1919 and been informed of them, it is highly doubtful he would ever have been convicted for the murder of Ben Sen Wu and his life would certainly have taken a dramatically different turn.

But even in 1966 he would have found *Miranda*'s safeguards useful had they been available to him. Wan's tribulations had not ended with his return to the land of his birth. The Chinese Communist Party, which had come to power in 1949, had embarked on a systematic persecution of "rightists" and "counterrevolutionaries" in which forced confessions were encouraged and trials were superfluous.

As it happened, even at age seventy-one Wan would have good reason to envy Ernesto Miranda his new protections.

Notes

1. Powell v. Alabama, 287 U.S. 45 (1932).
2. Brown v. Mississippi, 297 U.S. 278, (1936).
3. "Developments in the Law—Confessions," *Harvard Law Review* 79, no. 5 (1966): 962.
4. Anne Elizabeth Link, "Fifth Amendment—The Constitutionality of Custodial Confessions," *Journal of Criminal Law and Criminology* 82, no. 4 (1992): 878–903; Charles J. Ogletree, "Are Confessions Really Good for the Soul?: A Proposal to Mirandize 'Miranda,'" *Harvard Law Review* 100, no. 7 (May, 1987): 1826–45.
5. Ashcraft v. Tennessee, 322 U.S. 143 (1944). See also Yale Kamisar's 2011 speech, "The Rise, Fall and Decline of Miranda," October 18, 2011, University of Washington School of Law website, accessed January 28, 2016, http://www.law.washington.edu/multimedia/2011/YaleKamisar/Transcript.aspx.

6. Haynes v. Washington, 373 U.S. 503 (1963); Culombe v. Connecticut, 367 U.S. 568 (1961).

7. Culombe v. Connecticut, 367 U.S. 568 (1961).

8. Malloy v. Hogan, 378 U.S. 1 (1964).

9. For in- depth discussions of the evolution of tests for the admission of custodial confessions, see Anne Elizabeth Link, "Fifth Amendment—The Constitutionality of Custodial Confessions" *Journal of Criminal Law and Criminology* 82, no. 4 (1992): 878–903; Charles J. Ogletree, "Are Confessions Really Good for the Soul? A Proposal to Mirandize 'Miranda,'" *Harvard Law Review* 100, no. 7 (May 1987): 1826–45; Yale Kamisar, "A Dissent from the Miranda Dissents: Some Comments on the 'New' Fifth Amendment and the Old 'Voluntariness' Test," *Michigan Law Review* 65 (1966): 59–104; David A. Wollin, "Policing the Police: Should Miranda Violations Bear Fruit?" *Ohio State Law Journal* 53, no. 3 (1992): 812–19.

10. Miranda v. Arizona, 384 U.S. 436 (1966).

11. Miranda v. Arizona, 384 U.S. 436 (1966).

Reading 2.3

Brady/Giglio Disclosure Requirements
Where do They Start? Where do They End?

Randy Means and Pam McDonald

S UPREME COURT OPINIONS HAVE LAID THE foundation for police and prosecutors nationwide. Comprehensive federal policy now defines federal prosecutorial and law enforcement obligations. However, the instruction offered by lower courts to state and local law enforcement and prosecutors has been sketchy. Their practices are substantially affected by local conventions.

This article explains the fundamentals as defined by several Supreme Court opinions. Part Two will address gray areas. For example, whether relatively minor dishonesty requires disclosure, what degree of reliability must be established before an allegation of misconduct is discoverable, and when police personnel files more generally are subject to disclosure.

It will include a review of "model" policy provisions and relevant lower court decisions. Even though the "model" policies and many of the lower court decisions are not controlling authority for a particular police agency, a review of how they handle the more difficult issues is useful.

Brady and Giglio Fundamentals

The seminal Supreme Court case Brady v. Maryland (1963) held "that the suppression by the prosecution of evidence favorable to an accused upon request violates due process where the evidence is material either to guilt or to punishment, irrespective of the good faith or bad faith of the prosecution."

Brady was convicted of murder but the prosecution withheld a co-defendant's confession to the same murder. Subsequent cases clearly established that prosecutors have an affirmative duty to seek out exculpatory information known to others acting on behalf of the government (Kyles v. Whitley, 1995) and to disclose that information to the defense, even in the absence of a defense request (United States v. Agurs, 1976).

Exculpatory information is anything that casts doubt on the guilt of the defendant. Evidence is "material" under Brady only if there is a "reasonable probability" that disclosing it to the defense would have changed the result of the proceeding, and this "reasonable probability" of a different result is met when the prosecutor's evidentiary suppression "undermines confidence in the outcome of the trial" (United States v. Bagley, 1995).

Giglio v. United States (1972) extended the Brady rule to include any information that could be used to impeach the credibility of a prosecution witness, stating, "When the 'reliability of a given witness may well be determinative of guilt or innocence,' nondisclosure of evidence affecting credibility falls within (the Brady) rule" (citing Napue v. Illinois, 1959).

The prosecutor in Giglio failed to disclose the government's promise not to prosecute Giglio's accomplice in exchange for his testimony—the accomplice then gave key testimony implicating Giglio and falsely denying any agreement with the prosecutor. If the prosecutor had informed the defense about the agreement not to prosecute, the defense would have effectively impeached this essential government witness during his testimony.

The Supreme Court granted Giglio a new trial, declaring, "A new trial is required" if there is a reasonable likelihood that the false testimony could have affected the jury's decision (Giglio, 1972). A prosecutor's nondisclosure of Brady/Giglio evidence that is material to a finding of guilt constitutes reversible, constitutional error (see Bagley, 1995), and due process requires that the disclosure be made in sufficient time to permit the defense to use the information effectively at trial.

How Brady/Giglio Requirements Apply

When a police officer testifies as a government witness, the prosecutor has the same obligation as with other government witnesses to seek out and disclose Brady/Giglio information that casts doubt on the credibility of the testifying officer (Kyles, 1995), and police must give the prosecutor any impeachment information in their possession

Any Brady/Giglio information the police have is imputed to the prosecutor even if the prosecutor does not actually know of it, and police intentionally withholding information or "burying it in the file" may lead to police civil liability (see Tennison v. City and County of San Francisco, 9th Cir. 2009, and Carrillo v. County of Los Angeles, 9th Cir. 2015). The Supreme Court has confirmed the Brady rule is violated when the prosecutor fails to disclose even information that is "known only to police investigators and not to the prosecutor" (Youngblood v. West Virginia, 2006).

Some jurisdictions have developed rules in these regards through case law, statutes, and local rules. That is, New Hampshire Revised Statutes Annotated (RSA) Section 105:13-b specifically describes police personnel file disclosure requirements; in People v. Superior Court

(Johnson) (2015) 61 Cal.4th 696, the California Supreme Court reaffirms a state statute requiring prosecutors and defense to make a Pitchess (discovery) motion requesting judicial examination of police personnel files for exculpatory information.

Federal prosecutors and agents are controlled by rather comprehensive DOJ policy. Typically, police need to divulge crimes committed by officers, untruthfulness, and other dishonesty, and anything suggesting an officer's bias toward the defendant. Examples of possible but less-certain disclosure requirements are a history of excessive force or other misconduct, and concealing serious misconduct of other officers.

Just because the information is given to the prosecutor does not mean it will necessarily be given to the defense. The prosecutor makes the first determination of what qualifies as Brady/Giglio information, but when the prosecutor is unsure or reluctant to disclose specific information, the judge can review the information in camera (chambers) and decide what information merits disclosure to the defense. It is at this juncture—the judge's assessment—where many of the more worrisome incidents of minor or unverified police misbehavior are disallowed.

Police have an affirmative duty to locate potential Brady/Giglio material within their control and convey it to the prosecutor for their legal determination of what information must be disclosed to the defense, and when. Providing defense access to material, exculpatory information is part of assuring a fair trial, which is a defendant's constitutional right, and is therefore an ethical duty pursuant to promises made in a law enforcement officer's oath of office. Police will inevitably encounter areas where their responsibility is undefined or hazy. Especially in those cases, it may be useful to know how lower courts and others are thinking. More on this in Part Two!

Reading 2.4

Is Your Judge for Sale?

Andy Kroll

THE 30-SECOND TV SPOT IS STARK and brutal. First it shows the bespectacled face of candidate Louis Butler, then a grainy mug shot of an ex-con. "Louis Butler worked to put criminals on the street," the narrator warns, "like Reuben Lee Mitchell, who raped an 11-year-old girl with learning disabilities." After Mitchell's release from prison, the narrator continues, he raped again. "Can Wisconsin families feel safe with Louis Butler?"

This attack ad wasn't from a bitterly fought congressional race. It was from a 2008 campaign for state Supreme Court justice—a position that until recently was considered above the fray of partisan politics. Butler, the first African American Supreme Court justice in Wisconsin history, was defending his seat against a trial court judge whose campaign tactic recalled the GOP's infamous Willie Horton hit job on Michael Dukakis during the 1988 presidential campaign. Long before ascending to his state's highest court, Butler had been assigned as Reuben Lee Mitchell's public defender—he wasn't the judge in the case, as the nasty ad implied.

Butler's opponent, Michael Gableman, had been showered with campaign donations from business leaders, who were keenly aware of Butler's role in two decisions. One was a 4–3 ruling to strike down a $350,000 limit on so-called pain-and-suffering damages in malpractice suits. The other held that if an individual harmed by lead paint exposure couldn't identify the producer, then multiple paint companies could be held liable under a legal theory known as "risk contribution."

While Butler's and Gableman's campaigns spent a combined total of $1.2 million on the race, outside groups aligned with the US Chamber of Commerce and the state's labor unions spent $3.6 million, funding 89 percent of all the TV ads. Butler was the first sitting justice to get booted from the court in 40 years.

By 2011, with Wisconsin reeling from political battles over Gov. Scott Walker's union-busting agenda, the next Supreme Court race was equally ugly. This time it was conservative Justice

David Prosser defending his seat; a misleading ad from a partisan group backing his opponent claimed that Prosser, as a district attorney in 1978, had helped cover up sexual abuse of two young boys at the hands of a Catholic priest. (The abuse had only emerged years later; the victims called the ad "offensive, inaccurate, and out of context.")

Although Prosser successfully defended his seat, he says that the election—which saw nearly $5 million in total campaign spending—poisoned relationships on the court. The tension boiled over weeks later, when Prosser and Ann Walsh Bradley, a liberal justice, engaged in an argument that got physical as four of their fellow justices looked on. Bradley claimed Prosser choked her, while Prosser said he raised his hands in self-defense as Bradley charged at him. In police interviews, two conservative justices sided with Prosser, and two liberal justices with Bradley. Investigations by the county sheriff, the local DA, and a special independent prosecutor all cleared Prosser of any wrongdoing, but the controversy still festers. When I spoke with Prosser in September, written in chalk on the sidewalk outside the state Capitol was an invitation to visit him for "free chokes."

Bitter, costly judicial elections are by no means unique to Wisconsin. These days, as more candidates for the bench face rough contests—buffeted increasingly by outside money, thanks to the US Supreme Court's 2010 decision in *Citizens United*—state judges around the country often raise six- and seven-figure sums, mount statewide campaigns, and fend off attack ads from groups that don't disclose their donors. This trend has escalated over the last decade and a half as partisan groups realize that donating to judges can get them more influence, for less money, than bankrolling legislative campaigns. After all, the donors often end up with business before the very judges they are helping elect.

These are also the judges that most citizens who interact with the system have to face. Can Americans still trust in getting their fair day in court?

COURT CASES THAT make big news are usually in the federal system, where most judges are appointed by the president and confirmed by the Senate. Yet the vast majority of justice is done at the state level, where more than 100 million cases are filed annually (versus about 400,000 in federal courts). The nation's approximately 30,000 state court judges vastly outnumber their federal counterparts, and 85 percent of them will stand in at least one election during their career.

No two states pick their judges exactly the same way. Some hold partisan judicial elections, others have nonpartisan elections, and still others use merit selection—that's when legal experts select a short list of qualified candidates, the governor appoints one to the bench, and that judge later stands in a retention election.

The system has its roots in the Panic of 1837, a mini-depression fueled by rampant cronyism and massive overspending by corrupt governors and legislatures. Partisan elections replaced the tradition of elected officials appointing their friends to the bench, but for decades connections and loyalty still mattered most, with party bosses determining who won. Eventually states embraced nonpartisan elections and merit selection, and for most of the 20th century, judicial elections were a little-noticed corner of American politics.

Still, on occasion a contentious race attracted national attention. In 1977, Rose Bird became the first woman appointed to the California Supreme Court and its first female chief justice. An avowed foe of capital punishment, she voted to vacate all 61 death penalty verdicts that came before her, prompting Republican Gov. George Deukmejian to label her a "soft-on-crime liberal." With Bird up for retention in 1986, oil and agribusiness companies, which generally saw Bird's liberal views as a threat to their interests, poured more than $5.6 million into a campaign that would unseat her. It was an early glimpse of a reliable strategy for big business: Using the soft-on-crime theme to oust judges considered unfriendly to corporations.

Around that time, a political consultant by the name of Karl Rove was plotting his own assault on the Texas Supreme Court. Rove had helped launch the "tort wars" in response to what some Republicans saw as a court system too cozy with trial lawyers and too eager to slam corporations with hefty judgments that Rove had dubbed "junk lawsuits."

Running on the slogan "Clean Slate '88," conservative candidates backed by Rove's operation won five of the six open seats on the Texas Supreme Court. Not long after, Rove teamed up with the Business Council of Alabama to engineer a similar Republican take-over in that state.

Two years later, the US Chamber of Commerce, under the leadership of an aggressive new president named Tom Donohue, picked up on Rove's strategy. Pledging to "play hardball" against "frivolous" lawsuits, the Chamber spent $10 million on judicial races in 2000 alone. It pumped $4.4 million into Ohio's Supreme Court election—the largest expenditure from a single source on a court race in US history. In the following years, the Chamber injected tens of millions into races in Illinois, Michigan, Mississippi, and Wisconsin. Corporate America had grasped the potential to install friendly judges who could crack down on costly class actions and neutralize the efforts of consumer advocates. "We're clearly engaged in hand-to-hand combat," as Donohue put it, "and we've got to step it up if we're going to survive."

Unions spent millions on these races as well—particularly across the Upper Midwest, as labor leaders recognized they could get a great return on investment by backing justices sympathetic to workers' rights. As an official with the Ohio AFL-CIO once said: "We figured out a long time ago that it's easier to elect seven judges than to elect 132 legislators."

A major showdown came in 2004, in West Virginia's Supreme Court election. Don Blankenship, the former CEO of Massey Energy, donated $3 million to Republican candidate Brent Benjamin. Meanwhile, a nonprofit funded primarily by Massey Energy ran TV ads accusing incumbent Justice Warren McGraw of getting a child rapist out of prison and into a job at a high school. After Benjamin won, the investment paid off big time: He later cast the deciding vote to overturn a lower court's $50 million verdict against Massey Energy. Two years later, the US Supreme Court ruled that Benjamin should have recused himself. It overturned the decision and sent the case back to West Virginia. (Massey Energy ultimately prevailed in state court.)

Corporate interests also reaped a huge return on investment in the 2004 Supreme Court election in Illinois. Five years earlier, a jury had handed down a $1.19 billion penalty to the insurance company State Farm for requiring millions of claimants to accept subpar replacement auto parts. State Farm and its employees—working through the US Chamber, the Illinois Republican Party, and an Illinois-based tort reform group—steered $4 million to elect a sympathetic judge named Lloyd Karmeier to the Supreme Court, which was considering State Farm's appeal of the auto parts verdict. Karmeier, his opponent, and various outside groups spent a record $9.3 million on the race. Karmeier, who would later acknowledge that the sum was "obscene," won easily. And the millions State Farm spent were a pittance compared with what it gained: The next year, Karmeier cast the deciding vote to overturn the more than $1 billion verdict against State Farm.

Up to this point, the big spenders were mostly targeting contested judicial elections—ones in which a candidate challenged a sitting justice. Then came the Iowa Supreme Court's 2009 decision in *Varnum v. Brien*, in which the seven justices unanimously ruled that the state's ban on same-sex marriage violated the state constitution. Social-conservative groups leapt into action, targeting three of the seven justices who were up for retention election—ones where voters only check "yes" or "no." The National Organization for Marriage and its allies spent nearly $1 million and defeated all three. "They wanted to make sure we were punished for our decision and that other judges witnessed that so they wouldn't do it either," former Justice Marsha Ternus told me.

The strategy of turning sleepy retention elections into political showdowns has been spreading. In Florida's 2012 retention elections, the Koch-backed Americans for Prosperity and the Republican Party of Florida spent hundreds of thousands of dollars to unseat three sitting justices. A group called Defend Justice From Politics spent $3.1 million on the justices' behalf, helping them prevail. In Michigan in 2012, two anonymously funded nonprofits, the Judicial Crisis Network and Americans for Job Security, poured $2.1 million into attack ads against five judges on Michigan's 6th Circuit Court, though the judges won out. And earlier this year, Tennessee's lieutenant governor, Ron Ramsey, took it upon himself to spearhead an effort to unseat three sitting state Supreme Court justices—and, along with them, the attorney general, who is appointed by the court. Ramsey's PAC pumped $425,000 into a group running negative ads that blasted the three justices as "liberal on crime" and for "helping advance Obamacare." Funds were also contributed by Americans for Prosperity and the GOP's State Government Leadership Foundation, which said it planned to spend an additional $5 million in 2014 on judicial races in North Carolina, Tennessee, and elsewhere.

Though the three Tennessee justices prevailed in the end, one of them, Connie Clark, told me she's concerned about the precedent set by the fight. "As long as there are no limits on outside money," she says, "then this will become the new normal."

THE TRANSFORMATION of judicial campaigns has alarmed another veteran of the court system. "Judicial elections pose a serious threat," former US Supreme Court Justice Sandra Day O'Connor told *Mother Jones*. "If judicial decisions are in fact not fair and impartial—or even if they are perceived as being biased—the basis of support for our courts crumbles."

Initially, the 2011–12 election season—the first full cycle since *Citizens United*—saw a modest dip in overall reported spending on state judicial races, compared to four years earlier. But that is likely because much of the new spending does not have to be disclosed or tracked. This year, for example, Americans for Prosperity-Tennessee announced a "major new effort" to educate the public about the "liberal records" of the three justices—and not a penny of that spending was reported to the state. The outside spending on judicial races that we do know about rose to a record-high $24.9 million—a nearly sevenfold increase since 2000, and now accounting for 40 percent of the total spending on these campaigns.

Recent research suggests this flood of political money could be influencing judges' decisions. Emory University analyzed 2,345 state supreme court decisions from all 50 states between 2010 and 2012 and concluded that the more campaign money justices received from business interests, the more likely they were to vote in favor of businesses appearing before them. (Interestingly, the study found a stronger tie between business donations and Democratic justices' decisions. Republican justices, it speculated, were already more favorably inclined toward business interests, so the campaign money didn't make as much of a difference.) Another analysis, by the left-leaning think tank Center for American Progress, suggested that as more money was spent on soft-on-crime attack ads in campaigns, justices were increasingly siding with the prosecution.

The public may be starting to catch on: A 2013 poll by Justice at Stake, a nonprofit group focused on reforming the system, found that 87 percent of Americans believe that campaign donations could influence court rulings. "You can't expect judges to act like Huey Long on the campaign trail and expect them to be Solomon in the courtroom," says Bert Brandenburg, the group's executive director.

Some researchers dispute the notion that rough-and-tumble judicial elections are a problem. One recent Michigan State University study of supreme court races concluded that attack ads did not hurt incumbents in partisan elections. Other studies found that nonpartisan elections are less likely to draw a challenger, are less competitive even when there is a challenger, and attract fewer voters than partisan elections do.

The debate boils down to a fundamental notion: whether the judicial branch of government is unique from the other two and should be insulated from politics. With court integrity hanging in the balance, should judges be chosen the same way we pick presidents and members of Congress?

Randy Shepard, who served as the chief justice of the Indiana Supreme Court for 25 years, retired from the court in 2012 as the longest-serving state chief justice in American history. A lifelong Republican in a red state, Shepard has gone through the merit selection process and run in multiple elections. "What's at stake in these big-money elections is the promise of due process and an impartial court," he told me. "Do I as a citizen walk into that courtroom standing on a relatively level playing field?"

He offered up a hypothetical from a law review article he wrote that, he proudly noted, was cited by Justices Ruth Bader Ginsburg and Anthony Kennedy in the Massey Energy case—the one where the high court ruled that a judge who'd received massive campaign contributions connected to a company had to recuse himself from a case involving that company. "Say you're going before a trial judge making a decision about the custody of your grandchildren, and your evil son-in-law or daughter-in-law had made a very large contribution to the judge. How would you feel about that? You wouldn't feel very optimistic, would you?"

Section III

Exemplary Leadership and Challenges for Under-Represented Minorities in the Legal Field

Editor's Introduction

This last section of the anthology consists of readings that touch on various issues in the legal and criminal justice arena. They were chosen to inspire discussion, revelation, and compassion for the issues. At its essence, the law and criminal justice system is uniquely about wrestling with human problems, whether it is addiction, abuse, violence, or helplessness. It has been suggested that leadership training should begin as early as at the university. Leadership in this global world in which we live mandates an appreciation and understanding of other cultures, social mores, and the fluidity of illegality on the internet. It requires a flexible skill set and a deep appreciation for history in all its convergences to deal with our ever-changing world.

This section begins with an article that showcases a series of interviews with leaders in the criminal justice field. It is hoped that by reading their stories you will be inspired by their struggle, passion, and perseverance. Commissioner (ret.) Edward Davis was challenged repeatedly in his role as Chief of Police in Lowell, Massachusetts and when he was the Commissioner for the Boston Police Department. The first assignment as chief of the Lowell Police Department saw Davis grappling with an influx of diverse immigrants and the concomitant allegations of racial profiling. He addressed the problem immediately with Cambodian immigrants and both sides learned from each other. In his next post, as Commissioner of the Boston Police Department, Davis was on the frontlines, tasked with other agencies, to solve the Boston Marathon bombing. His leadership at that time, under extreme pressure to solve the bombing, is a testament to his grit and intelligence as a leader.

U.S. Marshal for Massachusetts John Gibbons was appointed as the first African American Marshal to Massachusetts by President Barack Obama. Gibbons grew up on the mean streets of Newark, New Jersey in a housing project. He excelled as a college student in Massachusetts and joined the Massachusetts State Police. His story is remarkable and displays his absolute dedication to his chosen career path. He began his path to leadership in his youth choir. His amiable and affable demeanor belie his street smarts and acuity of perception about people. He is a tough, resourceful leader, and his comments should encourage and inspire students.

Colonel (ret.) Marian McGovern was the first female colonel of the Massachusetts State Police. She handled some of the most heinous homicides in Massachusetts history. She has lectured around the world on interview techniques and taken advantage of every training and educational opportunity that presented itself. When she was appointed as the colonel, her peers applauded the appointment because she did indeed walk the walk, and talk the talk.

Superintendent Dr. Patricia Murphy runs a women's correctional facility. She is an intrepid leader in a field still dominated by men. She has introduced innovation and a systems approach to running this institution. She studied leadership from myriad perspectives and keeps abreast of new leadership styles. Dr. Murphy emphasizes leadership training for her correctional officers to ensure that her management team maintains the institution's reputation for innovative practices.

The legal field has seen an increase in under-represented minorities entering law school, and women now make up a slight majority of law school students; it has been a slow but steady ascension. The criminal justice field can do better in its outreach to minorities and women. Research has revealed that minorities in law enforcement are on parity with their percentage in the general population, but women are still woefully under-represented in law enforcement and corrections.

The second reading is about the first African-American U.S. State Supreme Court Justice Thurgood Marshall. It is no exaggeration when the author of this article calls him the "rock star of judges." This article should be required reading for students interested in law and the ability of the law to ameliorate wrongs.

The third article focuses on the challenges for women in policing. Many female students have apprehension about entering the male-dominated field of law enforcement. An acknowledgement that it is different for women is the reality. An honest dialogue is required. Women in the field can mentor those women entering the field. It is a rewarding and challenging career, but an appreciation of differences eases the path for new female officers.

Lastly, the fourth article in this section is about LGBT Oppression. College life is often a time when students are grappling with their sexual preferences. A college campus should be a place where all students feel safe. The reality that LGBT students are still abused needs to be understood by all campus personnel and incoming students. This reading is important in light of the U.S. Supreme Court's decision in *Obergefell v. Hodges*, 135 S. Ct. 2584 (2015). Once our law studies and criminal justice students graduate, they will interface with people from different races, ethnicities, genders, and sexual orientations. If you do not have compassion for *all* people, you should find a different career path.

Reading 3.1

Perspectives on Leadership
Massachusetts Law Enforcement Executives Address
Leadership Training

Alice Perry

L EADERSHIP AND HOW WE TRAIN NEW law enforcement leaders is profoundly important when examining bureaucratic function, and critical in times of economic upheaval, proposed innovation and policy implementation. Presently, the economic woes facing the United States demand that fiscal resources spent on police agencies reap the most benefit for the communities they serve.

We are currently in the problem-solving or preventive policing era in this country; it also includes community policing in its myriad forms. It has been a dramatic shift from traditional reactive policing used by police departments. The problem-solving approach requires police to consider problem solving as a primary goal, rather than simply reacting to situations after they have occurred. Law enforcement leaders must possess critical thinking skills, flexibility in problem solving and confidence that their subordinates have been schooled in leadership, ethics and integrity training.

This research is a follow-up to the quantitative research that consisted of a survey of Massachusetts's police chiefs and their attitudes, among other issues, as to when leadership training should begin. The majority of respondents in that survey believed that leadership training should begin in the police academy.[1]

This qualitative research consists of in-depth interviews with police leaders in a variety of Massachusetts law enforcement organizations; it was the author's intent to interview leaders from diverse backgrounds. Each police leader offered their opinion relative to the education and training they received on leadership. All of the police luminaries interviewed believed that leadership, ethics and integrity training should begin in the police academy. The interviews conclude with the police executives' suggestions on how to improve police leadership training.

Alice Perry, "Perspectives on Leadership: Massacusetts Law Enforcement Executives Address Leadership Training," *Police Forum*, vol. 24, no. 2, pp. 2-16. Copyright © 2014 by Academy of Criminal Justice Sciences. Reprinted with permission.

The four interviewees are: Former Boston Police Commissioner Edward Davis, United States Marshal John Gibbons, Colonel (ret.) Marian J. McGovern and Dr. Patricia Murphy.

The issue of police leadership is of paramount importance for a variety of reasons; chief among those is the global world in which we live with its varied cultures and diverse attitudes. We must cultivate leaders who have a global view buttressed by an ethical foundation that promotes efficacy in the delivery of police services, yet is steeped in respect for community members. Additionally, in this era of technological advancement and instantaneous communication, law enforcement leaders must be adept at the use of technology and must be prepared to answer a crisis with alacrity and impeccable communication skills.

Former Commissioner Edward Davis Boston Police Department

On April 15, 2013 two pressure cooker bombs exploded near the Boston Marathon's finish line; sadly, people died as a result of the bombing and hundreds were injured. A beautiful spring day and the annual Boston Marathon were eclipsed by the horror of the event. Former Boston Police Commissioner Edward Davis appeared on television repeatedly to explain the situation to Boston citizens and the nation's viewers. Davis was unflappable in his delivery as the situation unfolded. He calmed the city's citizens and mobilized the Boston police department's resources to deal with this tragedy. One can only marvel at his composure at a time when he must have been under enormous stress and pressure to solve the crime. The nation witnessed a leader in action. Davis stepped down as the Boston Police department commissioner in the fall of 2013. He is "currently on a fellowship at the Institute of Politics at Harvard, and he also recently announced he will be a security analyst for WBZ-TV."[2] Davis will be a board member with Mark43, a tech startup that will assist law enforcement agencies with software that will give them profiles of suspects and gang activity.[3]

In 2006, Edward Davis was named the Boston Police department's 40th police commissioner. Davis was born and raised in Lowell, Massachusetts. He began his law enforcement career in the Lowell Police department where he worked as a patrol officer, detective, and investigated narcotics and organized crime. He became police superintendent of the Lowell Police department in 1994.

Our interview takes place in a conference room in the Boston Police department when Davis was still the Boston Police department's police commissioner. Edward Davis is an imposing figure with a pleasant countenance but his demeanor and answers demonstrate a shrewd intellect. He explains that he spent ten years in the Lowell Police department running the Narcotics and Organized Crime division and during this time his leadership style was autocratic; he learned the style from his superiors. He believed that over time his management style had evolved into a democratic style of management. He attended a three-week leadership seminar at the Kennedy School of Government and was evaluated by his peers as to his management style. The results were tallied and he learned that his peers concluded that his management style was autocratic; he was genuinely taken aback, having concluded that he had evolved into a democratic leader. Davis, thus chagrined, undertook a period of self-study about leadership style and management. He also attended a number of leadership seminars. He is well versed in leading management theories and favors the book *The five pillars of total quality management* by Bill Creech.[4]

Creech was a four-star general whose book on management was well received; many corporations adopted his management principles. Creech wrote that, "Leadership is needed more than ever. As knowledge and attendant complexity grows, the more important, not less important, core values become. Also, complexity calls for even more efficient operation of the human system in every organization, regardless of type. And we know, from countless cases, that the human system does not work harmoniously or efficiently without enlightened, involved leadership—at all levels—that can pull the various disciplines together into an integrated product effort."[5]

Davis, believes, as Creech wrote, "... leaders build commitment through policies that increase motivation and decrease alienation. And leaders constantly probe for evidence of each. That requires involvement and sensitivity. It also requires trust, openness, and unfettered communication—not aloof, Olympian managerial detachment, as is so common in centralized organizations."[6]

Edward Davis, a proponent of problem-solving/community policing understands the difficulty in effectively using this model in police departments because police departments are centralized organizations. Problem-solving policing and community policing does require a decentralization of the law enforcement organization. The model envisions decision making by the officers and their supervisors out at their location whether that be a neighborhood police station or a storefront out in the community where the community policing team is located. This decentralization, it has been suggested, must include, and police executives must be responsive to, participatory management. Involvement in creating and implementing programs by the rank and file, as well as management will result not only in a cooperative, and knowledgeable department, but in one that is engaged.[7]

Davis was in charge of the Lowell Police Department when he put Creech's ideas into action with his outreach to Cambodian immigrants. Lowell, Massachusetts had a large manufacturing base before the factories closed. The population of similar mill towns suffered as a result of the loss of manufacturing jobs but Lowell's did not. During the 1980's and 1990's, the population in the city grew and was twenty percent more populated than it had been in 1980.[8] Most of the new population consisted of immigrants from all over the world, including Latin America, Asia and Africa.[9]

The influx of the diverse citizenry led to flare ups and tensions between the new immigrants and the police force. In 2000, there were cries of racial profiling and police superintendent Davis set out to address these concerns. The police department created a series of facilitated discussions with a group of representatives from each of the cities ethnic populations; this group was named the Lowell Race Relations Council.[10]

The biggest challenge to the police department was its relationship with the Cambodian community. After these Cambodian immigrants' experience with Pol Pot's Khmer Rouge genocide during the 1970's, they were understandably wary of the police. The group addressed such issues as cultural differences, gangs and traffic stops. "The council set itself five goals: education, communication, understanding, community unification, and generation of recommendations for the police department, all of which it continues to pursue at its monthly meetings and through follow-up with police and public officials."[11]

The police department and the council focused on the mutual education of each other. One council meeting featured an immigrant from Cameroon and a police officer acting out a traffic stop. The simulation revealed some potentially dangerous misunderstandings, for example, approaching the officer instead of remaining in the car when stopped. Council members were shown police training videos so that they could appreciate the concerns officers had during traffic stops. It was a success for the police leader's constituents. Everyone benefited. The United States Department of Justice awarded the Lowell police department grants that have allowed members of the department to train police departments around the country.[12]

Davis brought this concept of community outreach with him when he became commissioner of the Boston Police department. "The decentralization that has accompanied the movement to community policing in some cities has had the additional benefit of giving potential future chiefs on-the-job training as the commander of a full-service area or district station. In some departments, these local commanders have the responsibility for managing personnel, making assignments, dealing with media inquiries, and being responsible for crime."[13]

Davis believes that officers must get out of their cars and talk to people. "This is critical, says Davis, because we are only as good as the people we know and the depth of our relationship with the people in the community. More importantly, regarding problem-solving policing, if the officer on the street can identify the problems before they become crimes, we have accomplished our goal." Commissioner Davis, in addressing the importance of problem-solving policing expressed his frustration with the 'no-snitch' creed of the street, and says that the most troubling aspect is that members of the community have bought into that mentality.

This 'no-snitch' attitude frustrates law enforcement in the investigation of tragic homicides and violent crime. In an effort to combat that street code, he had stressed, to his department members and in the media, the importance of establishing trusting relationships with community members so that those with information can come forward without fear. He set up ways so that those looking to cooperate with the police could do so anonymously. He also partnered with the Boston District Attorney Daniel F. Conley in the establishment of a witness protection program.

Davis is earnest in his explanation of the importance of line level police officers making important decisions on the street. "This is not the military where sergeants are directing a platoon, the police officer is getting out of the car and they are making strategic and ethical decisions every day." He believes that the police academy should include leadership, ethics and integrity training. He believes that police academy training needs to lessen its military style of drilling and education and move to a balance between paramilitary training and team building.

Davis suggests that leadership training should include an explanation of transactional and transformational leadership style. "Management expert Bernard Bass, explains Davis, has written extensively on the transformational leader." Bass felt that transformational leadership could be learned and should be taught. Commissioner Davis believes in the combination of skills, both transactional and transformational. He believes that these management theories should be understood and mastered by leaders. "The goal, Davis posits, is to progress from the transactional style of leadership into a transformational leader."

"Transactional leaders are those who lead through social exchange. ... [t]ransactional business leaders offer financial rewards for productivity or deny rewards for lack of productivity. Transformational leaders, on the other hand, are those who stimulate and inspire followers to both achieve extraordinary outcomes, and, in the process, develop their own leadership capacity. Transformational leaders help followers grow and develop into leaders by responding to individual followers' needs by empowering them and by aligning the objectives and goals of the individual followers, the leader, the group, and the larger organization. More evidence has accumulated to demonstrate that transformational leadership can move followers to exceed expected performance, as well as lead to high levels of follower satisfaction and commitment to the group and the organization."[14]

Davis, if he had to design a curriculum for leadership and ethics training, would limit the number of lectures and would emphasize collaborative learning. He advocates role-playing and the use of case studies. He believes that the use of case studies is one of the best methods to teach leadership and ethics skills. He believes that mentoring in police departments is difficult but essential. He is an advocate of the International Chiefs of Police mentoring program whereby seasoned police chiefs mentor new chiefs. He is adamant that there must be a bridge between research and the practitioner.

Who was an inspirational leader to him? Janet Reno, the former United States Attorney General. He believes that Ms. Reno was an example of a team builder that Jim Collins' writes about in his bestseller *Good to great.*[15] Her success, Davis opines, is because she was able to transfer her street level skills to the Attorney General's office. "Reno," Davis explains, "was an inspiration because she had no ego and was constantly giving praise to her employees and developed a fierce loyalty from her staff. She also gave credit to others and was extremely intelligent."

Commissioner Davis in his role as Boston Police commissioner spent more than half his time as a police executive meeting with community groups and the media. In an effort to stay close to his staff, he was a believer in vertical staff meetings. Those meetings kept him up to date, he explained and infused his democratic style with new ideas and suggestions. His advice to new leaders is to stay abreast of new management theories, encourage input from subordinates and self-review your style. Davis concludes, "Leadership is about intellectual growth and being aware of the research being conducted around the world."

Dr. Patricia Murphy, Superintendent, Western Massachusetts Regional Women's Correctional Center

The entrance to the Women's Correctional Center in western Massachusetts is beautifully landscaped, and the squat brick building is hardly imposing. Dr. Patricia Murphy, the superintendent, meets me in the pristine lobby with a welcoming smile and a firm handshake. The only evidence that this is a correctional facility, and not the lobby of a business, is the correctional guard behind the reception desk.

Dr. Murphy's office, a short distance from the lobby, is brightly painted and laden with books and binders; she is a petite blonde with a reassuring yet resolute manner. Dr. Murphy tells me that she did not plan a career in law enforcement. She graduated with a bachelor's degree in education in the 1970's when there were no teaching jobs. She landed a position teaching for the Department of Youth Services in Massachusetts; this was a locked facility for youthful offenders. Her interest piqued, she returned to school for another Master's degree in special education. "I have always loved school," she laughingly comments.

In 1985, a new school, the Robert F. Kennedy (Action Corp.) School opened and needed a principal. The goal of principal had never occurred to her, but when the opportunity presented itself, she jumped on it. This school was a maximum-security treatment center. The school was one of many treatment centers, part of the non-profit organization started after the assassination of Senator Robert F. Kennedy. It used the behavioral management model and from the incipient stage, according to Dr. Murphy, it did two things right—it was well organized and it hired the right people from the day the doors opened.

Dr. Murphy describes her ten years at the school with wistful nostalgia, citing the commitment to make a difference the glue that bound the staff together; it was a tribute to the legacy of Robert F. Kennedy that inspired the staff.

In her position as principal, she was part of a team: with a clinical director and two program directors, under the leadership of a campus director. The school housed fifty-five of the most high-risk DYS kids, they had severe behavior problems and many had committed heinous crimes. At thirty-three years of age, Patricia Murphy, principal at this program began to make leadership decisions. She hired numerous teachers over the years and intuitively realized the importance of mentoring. She immediately commenced weekly staff meetings and tailored specific instruction where she felt her teachers needed it. She introduced orientation training as the first component in the mentoring process. Ms. Murphy, as a fledgling teacher, had had the benefit of mentoring when she started out and introduced programs for her teachers that underscored the importance of mentoring.

It was the training at the RFK School that she brought with her to her successive positions. The allure of more schooling beckoned and she commenced her doctoral work in 1981. Ms. Murphy received her doctorate from the University of Massachusetts; the focus of her study was influenced by Dr. Robert Sinclair, her department chair and Dr. Ralph Tyler of the University of Chicago; her area of expertise is curriculum development.

Dr. Murphy replied to an advertisement for an Assistant Deputy Superintendent for the Western Massachusetts Correctional Alcohol Center. The Center is run by the Hampden County Sheriff's Department in western Massachusetts. She had no contacts in the Sheriff's Department but the position interested her and she applied. She learned valuable leadership lessons from her mentors and believes that an important aspect of leadership is "starting from neutral. I work hard not to make assumptions from first impressions. Everyone gets one free pass on a small issue. You cannot start from a disciplinary perspective. It's important to teach staff to make the best decision for any given situation." Working in high pressure and stressful day-to-day environments, she also learned not to take things personally. Throughout her career she found it critical to take additional classes on leadership and organizational development.

Today, Dr. Murphy is the Superintendent at the Hampden County Sheriff's Women's Correctional Center (WCC) in Chicopee, Massachusetts using a systems approach. "Systems make everything run smoothly and provide consistency. If we, as leaders, provide consistency and continuity to staff, this translates to the work with inmates. Staff become confident in behavior management with the inmates resulting in making the inmates feel safe and 'safe' equals less acting out. In comparison, personality driven leadership only provides a roller coaster of results."

The institution amasses and analyzes data year round as part of the overall operation of the Sheriff's Department. The data and its analysis provide the foundation for the consistency and continuity in evaluation the overall performance of the facility.

Dr. Murphy encourages her staff, particularly the human services staff, to further their education. She has a training coordinator on staff and has a top-notch training program that she is very proud of. In the six years she has been the Superintendent of the Women's Correctional Center she has noted the growth of both middle management and line staff as mentors. When the WCC was being built, the Department hired one hundred and thirty-five new staff and had them undergo five weeks of training which included lengthy review of policy and procedures, security protocol, and gender responsive, trauma-based behavior management. The team spent the weeks training together at a local high school. The staff had two weeks together at the new facility before the inmates moved in. Safety was the number one priority—safety for the correctional officers, the inmates and staff.

Dr. Murphy is a proponent of mentoring. Her advice is to find an internal mentor and if none exists, find an external mentor. She believes that women need to understand their male peers by learning the language of the team—if you must, know your sports analogies she advises. She believes that education and training must be ongoing. Leaders need to be proficient in macro and micro strategies, understand the big picture and be detail-oriented. By all means, leaders must have a sense of humor and use it often.

Dr. Murphy is well versed in management theory but dislikes the use of the business model as the sole model in corrections. John Maxwell, a business guru; has had an influence on the Department; the Department's supervisory staff has watched many of his lectures. They have also been solidly influenced by Dr. Kevin Wright, author of *Excellence in correctional leadership*. He has evaluated the Sheriff's Department twice to assist them in improving their correctional model. She believes, "Jim Collins, the bestselling author of *Good to great* has found the perfect balance between business principles and a human services model." She applauds his tenet that the first step is to get the right people on the bus and then author a mission statement, not the other way around.[16]

Dr. Murphy and her staff authored the WCC mission statement after they had hired the transitional team: staff the Sheriff thought most reflected the goals of the Department who could complete all the planning for the opening of the new facility. The core mission statement includes an emphasis on public safety by being firm but fair. The mission statement's central theme is that everyone has an intrinsic dignity and should be treated with compassion; this statement guides the actions of this leader.

Marshal John Gibbons United States Marshal for Massachusetts

Marshal John Gibbons was the first African American marshal appointed by President Barack Obama. Marshal Gibbon's first exposure to leadership was as a junior deacon in his church, the Metropolitan Baptist Church in Newark, New Jersey. His father was a deacon and encouraged his son to participate. "Any shyness I had was eradicated as I had to lead the junior members in prayer and singing." John Gibbons was twelve years old when he started as a junior deacon.

John Gibbon's first mentor was his father who encouraged him to take a leadership role in the church but also encouraged his athleticism. John's father was a Newark police detective, his Cub Scout leader and coach for his athletic endeavors. John began running track at age eleven and started on the varsity football team at Southside High school in Newark as a sophomore and became the defensive captain. Gibbons believes that his high school football experience taught him the importance of team building and gave him insight into how a leader can motivate his team.

He learned that he could be a leader, by first, being an example to other team members. Second, he always volunteered for different assignments, third, he tried to be first in the drills, and fourth, the camaraderie of the team was strengthened by group activities like singing together which infused the group with spirit and motivation.

In his senior year in high school, Gibbons went to high school for the first half of the day and then attended Newark College for the rest of the day in the engineering tract. He discovered that though he excelled at math, he found engineering boring. He accepted a position on the football team at American International College and signed up for the pre-law major. In the mid-seventies, the college started a criminal justice program and Mr. Gibbons took a few courses and was hooked. He graduated with a bachelor's degree and immediately followed up with a Master's degree in criminal justice.

John Gibbons joined the Massachusetts State police in 1979 and knew that he would be on patrol for the first part of his career. However, his goal to be an investigator materialized at once when he was assigned to the Northampton barracks. He was writing and executing search warrants his first year out. He credits his first two supervisors with providing him with the guidance to grow as an investigator. Because it was a small office, Gibbons relates that, "There was no down time. There was no time for conflicts with other troopers because there was so much that needed to be done and we were a small office." Gibbons recalls that one of the most important classes in college, Human Relations, taught him the art of active listening. "It was this class that led to my success as an interviewer and investigator."

By the time he made the rank of sergeant, he was heading a narcotics bureau and authoring twenty search warrants a month. His leadership skills apparent, he was allowed to select the agents he wanted working with him and though he was an administrator he still made it a point to go out on calls with his investigators. During this time, he availed himself of training being offered by the Federal Bureau of Investigation. He attended an eleven-week course administered by the FBI on the management of an investigative unit. He attended schools put on by the Drug Enforcement Administration on interview techniques, drug conspiracy and racketeering cases. He was impressed by the federal seminars because they featured not only national speakers but speakers from around the world. He found diverse viewpoints contributed greatly to his outlook when dealing with criminal cases.

Gibbons' talents did not go unnoticed. He was awarded the Hampden County District Attorney's Law Enforcement Officer of the Year in 1995. He served as a supervisor of both federal and state gang and drug task forces. He graduated from the FBI National Academy 199th session, the DEA National Academy and the National Fire Academy. In 2006, he served as a committee member on the Newark, New Jersey Mayor Elect Cory Booker's Gang, Drugs and Violent Crime Policy Committee. In 2009, he served as President of the National Organization of Black Law Enforcement (NOBLE) Executives New England chapter.

John Gibbons sought out leadership opportunities through the National Organization of Black Law Enforcement. He embarked on a two-year leadership training program provided by NOBLE that was steeped in business management theory. Marshal Gibbons was a fast study and endorses business management principles; he believes that members of law enforcement should have more exposure to business courses and management theory.

Marshal Gibbons is enthused about the training he received through NOBLE. "It truly was invaluable," he says. Patrick Oliver, the former chief of police in Cleveland, ran the two-year Chief Executive Officer Mentoring program; the classes were held at Cedarville University in Ohio. There were only seven individuals in the program and all held high-ranking positions in their respective police departments; Gibbons was a Detective/Lieutenant with the Massachusetts State police at the time of the training.

"We were all assigned a mentor who worked with us over the course of the two year program. The lectures were terrific and we learned from the leader's stories. Because the program was small we were able to sit and really talk to one another and air our concerns; this was invaluable. In fact, when we started the program, one of the participants had just been promoted to chief so he told us about the first ninety days on the job and what was involved; those discussions were excellent."

John Gibbons was paired with Henry Whitehorn, who at the time, was colonel of the Louisiana State police. "His tutelage was motivating and inspiring. He had me accompany him to the Louisiana State House because he was involved in budget hearings; what a learning experience. He also had me sit in on executive meetings with his staff which was an education in and of itself. He was my mentor, he took that role seriously, and we became great friends."

When asked how he had grown or changed as a result of this mentoring program, John responded, "The NOBLE training opened my perspective on leadership because I was exposed to myriad leadership styles. I also heard from leaders from around the country and the various issues they were grappling with and this indisputably broadened my horizons. As far as practical application, it was serendipity that one of my fellow students had just been appointed chief because he explained to us "how to meet your staff." I took those lessons and applied them myself when I was appointed as the marshal for Massachusetts. I am responsible for four courthouses—two in Boston, one in Worcester and one in Springfield. I took the lessons learned from my NOBLE peers and incorporated them when I met my staff."

Some of his favorite courses were "Managing by Walking Around" which was taught by Patrick Oliver and "Taking Command" which was taught by retired General Frank Taylor. The first course encouraged those going into management positions to get out of their office and talk to their staff on a daily basis. This practice of 'managing by walking around' is highly successful in building relationships. As Gibbons points out, "If you stay in your office behind your desk, you don't know your people and what's going on."

Gibbons defines himself as an inclusive leader and makes a conscious effort to talk to all of his staff on a daily basis. He lists the attributes of a good leader: flexibility, being able to communicate effectively, and being able to lead by example; this includes an indefatigable work ethic. Gibbons goes on to explain that in law enforcement, where there is often a crisis followed by another crisis, leaders must be able to multitask. This ability to multitask must include being able to assess and prioritize efficaciously. In law enforcement, since much of it is predicated on responding to a crisis, a leader must be able to sustain the momentum and this means staying in top physical shape.

"If I were to design a leadership curriculum, I would include courses on Interviewing, Management Principles, Management by Walking Around, Budgeting, and Ethics. One of the most practical courses taught at the NOBLE training program was interview skills. "As you climb up the management ladder, interview skills become exceedingly important because you are competing with a small group of ably qualified candidates and you have to stand out. The training I received at NOBLE, especially Patrick Oliver's expertise, gave me the extra I needed in my interviews over the last couple of years."

"I believe that leadership training should begin in the academy. We must prepare the new members of law enforcement for their future and their future leadership opportunities. We must get them thinking about leadership from the beginning of their career."

"The leadership books I would recommend, and both are by James Maxwell, are *The question behind the question: Practicing personal accountability at work and in life* and *Developing the leader within you*."

What is his advice for future leaders? "Get in a position and do your best. Learn as much as you can and keep yourself open to all facets of the job by taking advantage of all training and further educational opportunities. "This job is all about partnerships and collaboration and cooperation but you can't have teamwork without communication. Ignore those ego-imposed territorial boundaries and reach across the aisle. I make it my daily mission to introduce local law enforcement to state law enforcement and local and state to federal law enforcement. This practice has resulted in relationships around the country and has allowed me to solve crimes that might not have otherwise been solved. Communication and collaboration carry the day."

Colonel (ret.) Marian J. McGovern, Massachusetts State Police

What an honor and what an achievement—Marian J. McGovern was the first female to lead the 144-year-old Massachusetts State Police; the oldest statewide law enforcement agency in the United States. Ms. McGovern was sworn in to head the police agency in January 2010. She retired in July 2012. When asked if it was difficult to be a female in the Massachusetts State police, she answered without hesitation and emphatically, "Yes! But it is not insurmountable."

Marian McGovern had never had any plans to join the state police. She was working as a small claims clerk in district court and the state police officers who came in encouraged her to take the civil service test. Recounting her time at the state police academy she says, "I didn't know what hit me." She fell in love with the job at the academy and remembers driving her cruiser home and taking it out for repeated drives because she was so thrilled to be riding in it. In 1979 she was one of nine women at the Massachusetts state police academy; today there are more than 170 women on the 2,250 member force.

McGovern started as a road trooper and ultimately moved up the ranks to detective. She spent twenty years in that role investigating some of the most violent crimes, including, child sexual assault, murder, drug trafficking and abduction cases. She began taking promotional exams and received her Master's degree in criminal justice in 1989 from Westfield State University. During her thirty year career she learned leadership skills from senior officers who mentored her. She recalls being influenced by a few leadership seminars that featured motivational speakers.

She thinks that leadership training should begin in the academy. She is fiercely proud of the Massachusetts State police training academy. She explains that the academy is broken down into three components. The first component is to break down the new recruits. The recruits are purposefully addled to see if they can withstand the chaos. Law enforcement is about moving from one crisis to another. The second component is teaching the recruits to respond to drill instructors and to learn to follow orders. The third, and most important component, is to foster team leaders. McGovern explains that this is the most fascinating aspect because it is astounding to see the recruits who are not team players and those that rise to the challenge and become team leaders.

McGovern believes that, "There should be standardized training at all Massachusetts police academies. The Massachusetts State Police training academy goes beyond the standard training. No one wants to be a part of something that is easy, and, no academy is easy, but we are readying them for doing the job they are expected to do, and, do it proficiently. Police officers have to make decisions in split seconds that will affect them, their community, their family and their organization. We have to make sure we are up to the task. We constantly ask, 'Are we training them the best way possible?' We need leaders who are not happy with the status quo in training. Crime changes. Now we are dealing with drive-by shootings. I never saw that when I started so leaders must constantly self-evaluate the training programs and practices."

She adds, "I believe leadership training should begin at the academy because we need to develop those individuals from the get go. You hope your recruits come in with the philosophy, 'I am here to serve the community.' That philosophy is the cornerstone of people who we see are future leaders. People exhibit traits of goodness, and, if they have that as part of their makeup, they make the right decisions for the right reasons. When good people make decisions for the greater good, and not for individual gain, they make the decisions for the right reasons."

Colonel McGovern taught leadership skills at the Massachusetts State Police academy. When asked about her favorite leadership books, she replies, "There are some great leadership books out there; I have an entire bookcase full of leadership books. I liked Steve Covey's books, Jack Welch's books, and the new release, *Lean In*. You need to pick one that matches your style because everyone's style is different. A book is not going to give you all the tools you need but you take different ideas from each one. I also liked Bill Belicheck's book; the Patriots, as a football team, are a great example in leadership."

Advice for recruits? "My advice for recruits is gain all the knowledge you can about this business and be passionate."

Are men and women treated the same? "No, McGovern answers, but we're close. Women have to do more work, and, as long as you know it, accept it, and do it. Women have shown they can do the job. Both male and female have to understand that law enforcement is involved in the cold, the benign, and the horrific. They are there when a baby is born by the side of the road and when a child is killed in a car crash. Both men and women *must* prove themselves out there. In law enforcement, in general, you must prove to one another that you can back each other up. You must have the physical tools, and mental and emotional abilities, to cope with the situation."

What is your advice for future leaders? "I would tell them a number of different things. First, we are in the era of intelligence-led policing. We must follow the numbers and use our commonsense. If it wasn't for analysis, we would not have found Osama bin Laden; the analysts found bin Laden."

"Second, I endorse the concept of 'Management by walking around.' There is a black hole where information doesn't go up or down. You have to know what is going on. It's mostly caused by people being overworked. That is why it is critical to get out of your office and go talk to the rank and file and find out what they're thinking. I found out that the mace holders were falling apart and the troopers were taping them together. I never would have known that but for the fact that I made it a point to talk to the troopers. This was a daily irritant for them and a big deal to them in their daily activities. By spending time with the front line, you find out their needs. Follow through with answers and solutions. If you don't, you lose your credibility. Follow up is so very important. If you don't really listen, don't ask the questions."

"Third, I never thought I would run the greatest law enforcement agency. The new ones coming up need to take the job, one assignment at a time. If you start the job looking to be the colonel, you miss everything along the way. Every role I took on, my goal was to be the best I could be every day, that is what propelled me into leadership roles. I was a team player and I earned respect. You can be a great test taker, but if you are not a team player, if you don't get your hands dirty, you will never garner respect and, as a leader, you are not going anywhere. I was always ready to take on any assignment and that has come back to reward me because people knew they could count on me. I was first in the office and the last to leave."

"Lastly, emulate those leaders you look up to and respect and understand what they do differently. Ask yourself—why do I like working for this sergeant but not that sergeant? Does he or she know the law? Does he or she listen? We all know bosses we would work with 24/7. If you are in a position of power, and you have a reputation as someone who never worked, you will never have respect. Do as I say, not do as I do, will never carry the day. There is no greater feeling than seeing your subordinates listen to you as a leader, not because you are the leader, but because they respect and trust you."

Conclusion

Police executives and policy-makers continue to grapple with how best to lead policing agencies into the 21st century. When should police organizations begin the development of prospective leaders? This is an issue that is currently fodder for debate and suggestion. In many states, police academy training is not standardized. Some members of law enforcement are sent to rigorous police academies that cover an extensive legal curriculum, ethics training, and have tough physical fitness requirements; other police academies are mediocre at best. We must continue to evaluate our training for prospective criminal justice leaders. The safety of the public demands that our resources be utilized so that law enforcement resources stay abreast of technology, best management and leadership practices; leadership training should begin in the police academy.

References

Bass, B.M. (2007). From transactional to transformational leadership: Learning to share the vision. Vecchio, R.P. (Ed.) (2007). In *Leadership: Understanding the dynamics of power and influence in organizations.* Notre Dame, IN: University of Notre Dame Press.

Bass, B.M. and Riggio, R.E. (2006). *Transformational leadership.* Mahwah, NJ: Lawrence Erlbaum Associates, Publishers.

Bass, B.M. and Steidlmeier (2004). Ethics, Character, and authentic transformational leadership behavior, pp. 175–196. In J.B. Ciulla (Ed.), *Ethics, the heart of leadership.* Westport, CT: Praeger Publishers.

Bass, B.M. (1990). *Bass and Stodgill's handbook of leadership: Theory, research and management applications.* New York: Free Press.

Breen, M.D. (1999). Today's leadership challenge for police executives. *Police Chief, 66.*

Burns, J.M. (2003). *Transforming leadership.* New York: Grove Press.

Ciulla, J.B. (Ed.) (2004). *Ethics, the heart of leadership.* Westport, CT: Praeger Publishers.

Collins, J. (2005). *Good to great and the social sectors: A monograph to accompany Good to great.* New York: HarperCollins Publishers.

Collins, J. (2001). *Good to great.* New York: HarperCollins Publishers.

Goldstein, H. (1990). *Problem oriented policing.* New York: McGraw-Hill.

Harris, D.A. (2005). *Good cops: The case for preventive policing.* New York: The New Press.

Mastrofski, S.D., Worden, R.E. and Snipes, J.B. (1995). *Law enforcement in a time of community policing.* Criminology, 33 (4).

Perry, A.E. (2010). *Continued utility of civil service for the chief's position.* The Police Chief, 8 (106–110).

Resig, M.D. and Parks, R.B. (2000). Community policing and the quality of life. In Skogan, W.G. (Ed.) (2004). *Community policing: Can it work?* Belmont, CA: Wadsworth/Thomson Learning.

Skogan, W.G. (Ed.) (2004). *Community policing: Can it work?* Belmont, CA: Wadsworth/Thomson Learning.

Wexler, C., Wycoff, M. and Fischer, C. (2007). *Good to great policing: Application of business management principles in the public sector.* U.S. Department of Justice Office of Community Oriented Policing Services. Washington, D.C.: Police Executive Research Forum.

Williams, E.J. (2003). *Structuring in community policing: Institutionalizing innovative change.* Police Practice and Research, 4 (2).

Notes

1. Perry, A. E. (2010). *Continued utility of civil service for the chief's position.* The Police Chief, August 2010, pp. 106–110.

2. *"Davis to join tech startup fighting crime,"* Boston Globe by Michael B. Farrell, February 27, 2014, p. B7, B11.

3. Ibid., p. B7.

4. Creech, B. (1994). *The five pillars of total quality management.* New York: Truman Talley Books/ Dutton.

5. Ibid., p. 329.

6. Ibid., p. 304.

7. Kelling, G. L. and Moore, M. H. (1988). The evolving strategy of policing. National Institute of Justice, Perspectives on Policing, vol. 4. In Kappeler, V. E. (Ed.) (1995). *The police and society.* Prospect Heights, IL: Waveland Press.

8. Ibid., p. 41.

9. Ibid., p. 42.

10. Ibid., p. 42.

11. Ibid., p. 43.

12. Ibid., p. 44.

13. Wexler, C., Wycoff, M. and Fischer, C. (2007). *Good to great policing: Application of business management principles in the public sector.* U.S. Department of Justice Office of Community Oriented Policing Services. Washington, D.C.: Police Executive Research Forum, p. 19.

14. Deluga, R. J. and Souza, J. (1991). The effect of transformational and transactional leadership style on the influencing behavior of subordinate police officers. *Journal of Occupational Psychology,* 64, pp. 49–55.

15. Collins, J. (2001). *Good to great.* New York, NY: Harper Collins Publishers.

16. Jim Collins authored a monograph for social sector leaders. Collins, J. (2005). *Good to great and the social sectors: A monograph to accompany Good to great.* New York, NY: HarperCollins Publishers.

Reading 3.2

Lawyer of the Century
Thurgood Marshall's Legacy Looms Large in a World He Helped Create

Brian Gilmore

MORE THAN ANY OTHER SUPREME COURT Justice, Thurgood Marshall was the equivalent of a legal rock star in America.

"Only Marshall was so often accosted by admirers that he found it difficult to dine in public," John C. Jeffries Jr. wrote in his 1994 biography of Marshall's Supreme Court colleague Lewis F. Powell Jr. "Only Marshall would find himself played by the elegant Sidney Poitier in a television mini-series," and only Marshall would be celebrated today even if "he had never been named to the Supreme Court."

Marshall achieved his exalted stature on merit. The country was changed forever by the legal assault he led against legalized American racism from the 1930s through the late 1950s. One hundred years after his birth, he is remembered as arguably the most important lawyer of the 20th century. And there is no shortage of tributes standing in testimony to his importance.

In 2005, the state of Maryland officially renamed the airport serving his hometown Baltimore/Washington International Thurgood Marshall Airport (BWI). Schools and streets across the country bear Marshall's name. And just recently, the legendary jurist reached the bright lights of Broadway with Tony Award-winning actor Laurence Fishburne starring in *Thurgood*, a critically acclaimed one-man show at the historic Booth Theatre.

Marshall's path to immortality began across from a Baltimore slaughter pen, where he was delivered by midwife on July 2, 1908. He was born to William and Norma Marshall, proud middle-class Blacks who brought their new addition into a world of racial turbulence. Twelve years earlier, the U.S. Supreme Court declared its approval of racial apartheid ("separate but equal") in America in *Plessy v. Ferguson*. Segregation was the norm in the Baltimore of Marshall's youth, as was racial violence.

Marshall, growing up as part of an extended family aware of and practical about America's racial madness, spent his early years familiar with racism but largely oblivious to the struggle to overcome it.

In his 1993 book, *Dream Makers, Dream Breakers: The World of Justice Thurgood Marshall*, Carl T. Rowan noted that Marshall spent his youth "goofing off," "driving his mother crazy" and "showing no signs whatsoever that he was destined for a leadership role in combating the racism and the atrocities that seared the minds of his older relatives." The future Supreme Court justice graduated from high school only because his teachers wanted to appease his mother, Rowan wrote.

After high school, Marshall attended Lincoln University in Pennsylvania, where he spent much of his time chasing women, guzzling alcohol and shunning scholarship.

It was only after graduating from Lincoln and entering Howard University School of Law that he found his way in the world. Marshall quickly came under the influence of Charles Hamilton Houston, the school's immortal dean, a "perfectionist" Marshall would come to regard as "one of the greatest lawyers" he had been privileged to know.

Houston was determined not only to produce lawyers who would destroy America's racial apartheid system but also to fashion Howard into an institution that would produce such lawyers for generations. Marshall, one of the first to emerge from Houston's rigorous system, was to be the prototype.

Not long after graduating from law school in 1933, Marshall found himself working as a trusted associate at the center of Houston's campaign to vanquish segregation through the courts. Marshall achieved his first major legal victory in 1936, when he successfully sued to help a Black man, Donald Murray, gain admission to the University of Maryland Law School. When Maryland's Court of Appeals ordered Murray admitted, it was sweet revenge for Marshall, who had been denied admission because of his race.

That first major victory was followed over the next 25 years by one landmark case after another attacking various aspects of the systematic racism Marshall first encountered as a boy. Marshall built his reputation as one of the nation's foremost lawyers by making full use of his well-developed people skills and his ability to spin a tale.

"He had the ability to listen and to absorb great legal minds and present what they said in a way that anyone

Marshall speaks to reporters in Washington, D.C., on Aug. 28, 1958 (top) and arrives in Nairobi, Kenya on July 10, 1963 (bottom).

Marshall's family joins him at the U.S. Supreme Court.

could understand," Julian Dugas, a member of the *Brown v. Board of Education* legal team and an adjunct professor at the Howard University School of Law, told *The Crisis*.

In 1940, Marshall won the first of his 29 Supreme Court victories in *Chambers v. Florida*. A unanimous court threw out convictions of four Black men coerced into confessing to crimes they didn't commit in a case regarded as one of the key building blocks of the due-process rights Americans enjoy today.

Next up was the 1944 case *Smith v. Allwright,* in which the Court declared illegal the all-White primary system sponsored by the Democratic Party of Texas. Marshall by then had been appointed chief counsel to the NAACP Legal Defense and Educational Fund (LDF), a post he held from 1938 through 1961.

In 1948, Marshall helped end racially restrictive housing covenants (in *Shelley v. Kraemer*) and in 1950 he led the way (*Sweatt v. Painter*) in bringing down the Texas state system of separate law schools for Blacks and Whites. These triumphs led to the most important victory of all—the *Brown v. Board of Education* decision of 1954.

Brown encompassed five cases on which the best and the brightest civil rights lawyers worked tirelessly for years. In the end, however, it was Marshall who put the victory together, Jack Greenberg, former chief counsel of the LDF, told *The Crisis*.

"He was, most people agree, the commander-in-chief of the *Brown* case," Greenberg said.

The court's May 17, 1954, decision in *Brown* overturned the 1896 *Plessy* decision and initiated the racial transformation of America.

"We conclude that in the field of public education the doctrine of 'separate but equal' has no place," Chief Justice Earl Warren famously wrote for a unanimous court. That legal earthquake led to more victories for Marshall and his associates.

In 1961, President John F. Kennedy tapped Marshall to become a U.S. Appeals Court judge for the 2nd Circuit in New York. Marshall accepted the post with gratitude and wrote 112 opinions while he served. Not one got reversed.

Laurence Fishburne portrays Marshall on Broadway.

On July 13, 1965, President Lyndon Johnson nominated Marshall to become the 33rd Solicitor General of the United States, entrusting him with responsibility for arguing the government's position in Supreme Court cases. With the civil rights struggle raging in the streets of America, the position gave Marshall an opportunity to argue in important cases that affected the movement.

Considering Marshall's unparalleled contributions as the legal champion of that movement, his nomination to become the first African American Supreme Court Justice seemed a fitting culmination to an epic career. President Johnson named Marshall to the high court on June 13, 1967, famously proclaiming it was "the right thing to do, the right time to do it, the right man and the right place." Despite some fierce opposition from Southern Democrats, Marshall was confirmed on Aug. 30, 1967 by a vote of 69–11.

As a justice, Marshall helped uphold the more liberal wing of the court in the face of a rightward shift in the 1970s. In *Making Constitutional Law,* his book about Marshall's service on the court, Mark Tushnet aptly describes him as a "Great Society liberal" and a justice who "supported the expansive use of national power, especially legislative and judicial, particularly on behalf of minorities and claims for traditional civil liberties." Marshall's opinions and dissents reflect that desire to empower ordinary citizens and the poor.

He also distinguished himself in capital punishment cases.

Gay Gellhorn, a retired law professor who was a clerk to Marshall during the 1983–84 session after capital punishment was legally reinstated, noted that Marshall always dissented in such cases and describes him as "an independent thinker" and a "great storyteller."

"We spent many nights poring over last-minute death penalty petitions," Gellhorn told *The Crisis*.

Marshall served on the court for 24 years, retiring in 1991.

His centennial has occasioned new critical examinations of his career and new expressions of admiration. *Exporting American Dreams: Thurgood Marshall's African Journey*, by University of Southern California law professor Mary L. Dudziak, details his role in drafting a Bill of Rights for Kenya, which became an independent African nation in 1963.

"We tend to cabin American civil rights figures into a domestic story," Dudziak told *The Crisis*, "but Marshall and the impact of his work are best understood by also paying attention to his engagement and impact beyond American borders."

Thurgood, the Broadway production, mines rich storytelling from its subject's colorful life. In a Q&A session after a performance, Fishburne called the play an "annuity"—offering a role he will have the opportunity to play for the "next 20 years." Each performance, he said, will educate more and more people about Marshall's story. "I get to reach generations," he added. A film version is in the works.

There is no shortage of drama in modern America, with its complicated blend of dispiriting setbacks and inspirational leaps forward. One can't help but wonder what Marshall would think of today's complex and fast-moving society, one that he helped create. Jack Greenberg ventured to guess that he would hate the "regression into segregation" and the persistence of "Black ghettos." Laurence Fishburne said he might find reason to be upbeat as well. Reflecting on Barack Obama's rise, the actor said, "I think he would raise a glass to that."

Thurgood Marshall Jr., a lawyer himself, offered a thoughtful perspective. "My father was always restless and always agitating for change. So for all the positives he would find today, he would also surely see that there is much unfinished business, particularly with regard to equal opportunity. Yet he was always hopeful that our better nature would continue to bring improvements."

Brian Gilmore teaches in the Clinical Law Center at the Howard University School of Law.

Reading 3.3

Challenges for Women in Policing
How Law Enforcement Culture can Become More Gender-neutral

Shannon Woolsey

I T HAS BEEN 100 YEARS SINCE Alice Stebbin Wells became the first woman to be known as a "police woman" when she joined the Los Angeles Police Department in 1910. She handled cases involving women, juveniles and children. There has been some dispute over who actually was the first female police officer due to the fact that early women in policing had such varied job tasks and did not do street patrol.

They were often viewed as mothers with badges. Some of their early duties involved patrolling dance halls to keep tango dancers at least 10 inches apart and patrolling beaches to stop clandestine activity. By the early 1960s, about 2,400 women were serving municipal police departments in the United States.

It was not until 1968 that the Indianapolis Police Department made history by assigning two female police officers to patrol on an equal status with male counterparts. Following the women's movement and the passage of the Equal Opportunity Employment Act in the 1970s, more women began entering the field of law enforcement.

It was predicted by researchers in the late 1980s that by the turn of the 21st century, the number of women in law enforcement would reach nearly 50 percent of the workforce. Those predictions never materialized. The growth of women in policing has progressed slowly and has not shown significant gains during the last several years. In 2008, according to the Census Bureau, there were 99,000 female police officers out of approximately 884,000 officers, which is 11 percent of policing.

Numerous studies have been completed since the 1970s when women were first entering the field of law enforcement. The studies revealed time and time again that women can and do perform all the duties of patrol officers, and also excel in many areas. The question of physical strength continues to emerge when the issues of female police officers are brought up; however,

Shannon Woolsey, "Challenges for Women in Policing," *Law & Order*, vol. 58, no. 10, pp. 78-80, 82. Copyright © 2010 by Hendon Publishing Company. Reprinted with permission. Provided by ProQuest LLC. All rights reserved.

physical strength has not been shown to predict either general police effectiveness or the ability to be successful in handling dangerous situations. Nor has physical strength been shown to play a role in line-of-duty deaths. Most police fatalities are related to gunfire and automobile accidents.

Studies have shown that women in policing are less likely to use excessive and deadly force. They are also less likely than their male coworkers to be involved in fights or acts of aggres-

sion on the job. Female officers rely more on interpersonal skills than physical force. Women are known to deescalate potentially violent situations more often than men. This emphasis on communication goes a long way in the modern approach to policing known as "community policing." Police departments are leaning more toward community partnerships and proactive problem-solving versus the "tough guy" reactive approach popular in years past.

Research supports that women do experience unique workplace stressors and issues, such as language harassment, sex discrimination and a lack of mentors/role models. Additional barriers that have been identified are double standards and the issue of balancing family with career. The primary deterrent to women entering the field of law enforcement remains the icy welcome they receive from some of their male colleagues. Women face certain psychological pressures not encountered by men.

Peer acceptance is one of the greatest pressures operating within police organizations. The desire to be known as a "good officer" is a strong motivating factor, and failure to achieve that status can be very demoralizing and devastating. Unlike their male counterparts, women must overcome the societal prejudice of being known as the "weaker sex." Many female officers also report feeling they have to work twice as hard to prove themselves and to be accepted, whereas male officers can just show up and gain acceptance.

Entrance exams for police jobs often require tests of physical agility, and some have been considered gender-biased. Some departments have required the scaling of a 5- or 6-foot solid wall, which requires great upper body strength and may keep many women from passing,

no matter how strong or agile they are. Certain departments are revising their physical entrance exams, realizing that the 5- or 6-foot solid walls are discriminatory and in need of review.

The women who could scale such a wall would be so drained of energy, they would likely find it difficult to complete the rest of the test in the allotted time-frame. Some changes being made to the agility testing allow for two foot braces providing foot leverage, making it easier to scale the wall, as well as more realistic.

Sexual harassment is also a primary area of concern and more prevalent in male-dominated workplaces. In November of 2008, a female officer in the LAPD canine bomb unit was awarded $2.25 million in a sexual harassment lawsuit, stating that male members of the unit exposed their genitalia, made inappropriate remarks and excluded her from training opportunities (*Patricia Fuller v. City of Los Angeles*).

To make matters worse, LAPD paid out an additional $3.6 million to a male member of the same unit who was the only person to come to the defense of the harassed woman. The 21-year veteran suffered retaliation by being stripped of his rank and kicked out of the elite unit (*Donald Bender v. City of Los Angeles*).

Legal opinions from federal court cases have indicated that a code of silence often exists in these types of cases. Preliminary results showed that subjects who report incidents of sexual harassment may be subjected to a variety of retaliatory behavior designed to deter them from reporting illicit behaviors. The retaliatory behavior is often in the form of shunning, isolating and ostracizing the victim; failing to provide backup in critical

situations; and refusing to communicate or cooperate with the victim on assignments. This type of behavior manifests in preventing or delaying victim reporting and reinforces the code of silence.

This sends a clear message about the treatment the victim should expect to receive if a report is made. The practice of hiring and retaining more women will lessen a department's liability by reducing the numeric underrepresentation of female officers. An increased number of women can have a definite impact on reducing the climate of sexual harassment and gender discrimination.

Yet another deterrent for female police is balancing family and work, as well as pregnancy. Women who are considering a career in law enforcement need to know that, should they choose to become a mother, their job will not be in jeopardy. The Federal Pregnancy Discrimination Act requires employers to treat women affected by pregnancy, childbirth or related conditions the same as other persons who are not affected but are similar in their ability or inability to work. The act is designed to guarantee women the right to participate fully and equally in the workplace while also not denying them the right to have a family.

The most important step a department can take is to have a comprehensive policy regarding pregnancy made available to all female employees. The policy should address the Family Medical Leave Act, a light duty policy, disability insurance and paid leave issues, as well as uniform modifications and firearm qualification adjustments due to potential lead poisoning. Pregnancy is a part of life for many women; employers who fail to accommodate the combined demands of work and pregnancy threaten to rescind decades of advances for women in the workplace.

Police work remains a male-dominated field; however, many progressive police chiefs would like to hire more women but are finding a shortage of qualified applicants. In order for the pool of qualified women to increase, agencies need to send a clear message that women are welcome and will be valued. Some departments are going as far as specifically recruiting female officers.

Consent decrees remain one of the most valuable tools for increasing the number of women in law enforcement. Studies show that they are associated with a pace of progress double that of agencies without such decrees. Furthermore, studies have shown that when such consent decrees expire, that growth slows considerably in many cases. Consent decrees may be necessary until police departments are willing and capable of successfully hiring and retaining females.

Instituting a mentor program can go a long way in retaining female officers. Some women in smaller departments are entering as the only female in the department. This can make it more difficult to succeed knowing women face challenges and obstacles that their male colleagues do not. To alleviate this feeling of isolation, researchers recommend mentoring programs. They can be formal or informal.

Mentoring operates under the assumption that people relate more positively and readily to peer assistance than to supervisory direction. It provides an atmosphere for non-threatening growth and learning opportunities. The benefits of a mentoring program are extensive and include improved job performance, increased cohesiveness and cooperation, and improved morale of female officers.

With the cost of hiring, training and retaining a new employee estimated at about $40,000, it is beneficial to departments to utilize every tool available to keep new employees. An additional benefit of mentoring is that it can greatly reduce liability by providing a support system to resolve sexual harassment or gender complaints before they escalate into costly law suits.

Regardless of the type of mentoring program chosen by a department, the goal is to encourage one-to-one partnerships which cultivate professional growth for the individual, the department and the community, while reducing the costs associated with attrition.

The goal of a progressive police department should always be to recruit and retain a quality group of officers who reflect and represent the community they serve. This should include women and other minorities. The 21st century police officer is one who embodies not only physical strength, but also strength in character, communication and problem solving. The ideal officer is neither male nor female but a combination of admirable and reputable traits that embody what our communities desire in the new age of policing.

It is time to redefine the outdated image of male police officers who are unapproachable and defined primarily by their prowess. Both genders bring exceptional qualities to policing that, when combined, provide for excellent service and infinite wisdom.

Police departments should take the necessary measures to ensure that they provide that mix of qualities by recruiting and retaining quality female candidates. They should involve male officers in the mentoring process who outwardly exhibit the acceptance necessary to provide a supportive learning and working environment for women. Furthermore, they should implement supportive and clear sexual harassment and pregnancy policies. The question is no longer whether women should be in law enforcement, but when their representation will be sufficient.

Reading 3.4

LGBT Oppression

Sandy Watson and Ted Miller

My Back Pages

Yes, my guard stood hard
when abstract threats
Too noble to neglect
Deceived me into thinking
I had something to protect
Good and bad, I define these terms
Quite clear, no doubt, somehow.
Ah, but I was so much older then,
I'm younger than that now.
(Bob Dylan, 1964)

I kept myself to myself so I got the grief of being bullied. I twice nearly killed myself because of the bullying ... I still get the usual, "Hey puffer ... what u doing still alive?" And crap like that. (Gary, n.d.)

When I started to realize in 5th grade that being gay wasn't accepted, and that most people believed it wasn't real, I started my hiding. (Cody, n.d.)

I want to come out of the closet but I'm too scared. My whole school is filled with people that just take the piss out of gays and I wouldn't be able to stand it. (Dani, n.d.)

Sandy Watson and Ted Miller, "LGBT Oppression," *Multicultural Education*, vol. 19, no. 4, pp. 2-7. Copyright © 2012 by Caddo Gap Press. Reprinted with permission. Provided by ProQuest LLC. All rights reserved.

T HERE IS NO QUESTION THAT LESBIAN, Gay, Bisexual, and Transgender (LGBT) students are routinely verbally, emotionally, and physically bullied by their classmates in school contexts as the aforementioned statements from a gay student internet message board demonstrate (Meyer, 2008; Nansel et al., 2001; Pellegrini, Bartini, & Brooks, 2001; Stockdale, Hangaduambo, Duys, Larson, & Sarvela, 2002; U.S. Department of Education and U.S. Department of Justice, 2006).

Just how often LGBT students suffer abuse at the hands of their peers in schools varies across studies cited in the literature since the issue was first explored in the early 1990s. Human Rights Watch (2001) concluded that as many as two million U.S. students have been harassed by peers at school due to their sexual orientation, while the Gay Lesbian Straight Educational Network (GLSEN) National School Climate Survey (NSCS, 2005) results indicated that approximately 75% of students reported hearing anti-gay slurs used by their peers (such as "dyke" and "faggot") regularly in the school setting. In fact, the results indicated that approximately 90% of students frequently heard their peers utter the expressions "that's so gay" or "you're so gay" during the course of every school day.

Further, over one-third of students reported that they had personally experienced verbal or gestural harassment at the hands of their school peers based on their sexual orientation and over 25% indicated experiencing physical abuse (as examples, getting spit on, being chased by other students in their cars in the school parking lot, being touched or grabbed inappropriately) by their classmates. More alarming, approximately 38% of students reported experiencing incidents of physical assault at school simply because of their sexual orientation (GLSEN NSCS, 2005). Physical assaults reported run the gamut from getting shoved into lockers, pushed down stairs, beat up, and even shot.

One of the prevailing reasons why LGBT students perceive their schools to be unsafe is that many of their teachers do not intervene when they (the teachers) witness peer-on-peer LGBT bullying and harassment, effectively allowing the berating and or violent behaviors to continue. One alarming report indicated, "... teachers fail to intervene in 97% of incidents involving anti-gay slurs at school" (Carter, 1997).

Recently, Kosciw and Diaz (2006) stated that 83% of LGBT students report that their teachers rarely, if ever, intervened when students made homophobic remarks. Teachers who turn a deaf ear to anti-LGBT harassment directed toward one student by another, who don't take corrective action when LGBT students report peers' acts of violence inflicted upon them, and who don't intervene when they witness acts of violence against LGBT students are complicit in their silence.

These actions from authority sanction the harassers dehumanizing treatment of LGBT peers and convey that the behaviors are not only acceptable, but welcome (Buston & Hart, 2001; Jordan, Vaughan, & Woodworth, 1997; Kosciw & Cullen, 2001). Shor and Freire (1987) stated:

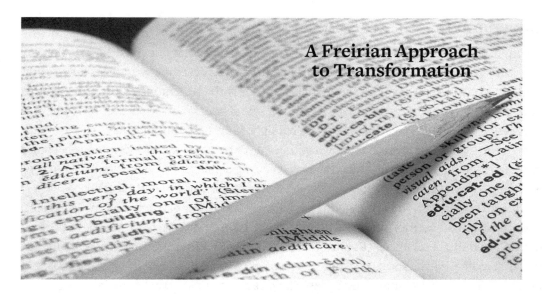

A Freirian Approach to Transformation

The ideology of the 'neutral' teacher fits in, then, with support for the status quo, because society itself is not benign. Consciousness is not a blank page; school and society are not neutral fields of social equals. Not acknowledging or not challenging inequality in society is to cooperate in hiding reality, hiding conditions that would weaken dominate ideology. The teacher who pretends that reality is not problematic thus reduces the students' own power to perceive and to act on social issues. An opaque reality diempowers people, by holding a screen in front of what they need to see to begin transformation. 'Neutral' teaching is another name for an opaque curriculum, and an opaque curriculum is another name for a domesticating education. (p. 174)

According to Meyer (2008) many studies (Buston & Hart, 2001; California Safe Schools Coaltion, 2004; Chambers, van Loon, & Tincknell, 2004; GLSEN and Harris Interactive 2005; Kosciw & Cullen, 2001; Peters, 2003; Renold, 2000; Wilson, Griffin & Wren, 2005), have shown that homophobic harassment has become "… accepted parts of school culture where faculty and staff rarely or never intervene" (p. 555). This has happened despite the fact that in 2003 a federal appeals court ruled that schools can be held liable when they do not intervene in the harassment of LGBT students (*Flores v Morgan Hill Unified School District*, 2003).

When peer-on-peer verbal and gestural anti-LGBT harassment is allowed to continue because teachers and administrators choose not to intervene, the chances of such abuse escalating into physical harassment and assault increases dramatically (Human Rights Watch, 2001). Paulo Freire stated, "Washing one's hands of the conflict between the powerful and the powerless means to side with the powerful, not to be neutral."

Understanding the (Mis)Behavior

To understand why LGBT harassment and abuse is so prevalent one must explore the way one thinks about sexuality and how the societal norms regarding sexuality came about. Gender scholars such as queer theorists posit "... it is the hegemony of heteronormative patriarchy that constructs dominant notions of sex, gender, and sexual orientation in very oppressive ways" (Meyer, 2008, p. 556). What light to cast an examination of the phenomenon in? Foucault (1978) stated that when one way of being is cast as "normal," it becomes privileged and legitimized, and all other ways of being default to "deviance" and "deviance" is often perceived as taboo, other, abnormal, unacceptable, and/or pathological.

Queer theory proclaims that heterosexuality is socially constructed as the prevalent, natural sexual orientation and thus does not call attention to itself, allowing it to become invisible and unquestionable (Robinson & Ferjola, 2008). Heteronormativity is an institution that maintains the status quo and "... keeps people in their places" (Blackburn & Smith, 2010). Atkinson and DePalma (2008) describe it as a "... tautology that explains things must be this way because that's the way they are" (p. 27). Rich (1980) casts the heteronomative institution as oppressive, and likens it to classism and racism.

When one way of existence is accepted as natural and normal (in this case heteronormativity), then, unless evidence exists or statements are made to indicate otherwise, all people are generally thought to exist within those constructs of heteronormativity. Thus, in keeping with queer theory, and Foucault's thoughts on deviance in the school setting, students who are perceived as existing within the "normalcy" of heterosexuality are invisible; they are not harassed, abused, or assaulted by teachers or peers for being heterosexual. Openly LGBT students however, (and those perceived to be so, correctly or not) because they are not sheltered within the invisible safety net of heteronormativity, are subject to identification as deviants, resulting in an increased potential for harassment, abuse, and or assault by their peers and teachers (Rich, 1980).

It is really no surprise, therefore, why so many teachers fail to intervene when LGBT students suffer harassment and abuse at the hands of their peers and why many teachers even participate in such harassment because the very institutions who employ teachers serve to "... enforce the institution of heteronormativity" (Blackburn & Smith, 2010). From as early as the pre-kindergarten years, students are subject to a variety of routines, procedures, curricula, and pedagogy that enforce heteronormativity to include gender segregation, gender role enforcement, exposure to literature in which heterosexuality is centrally positioned, and the heteronormative performances of school faculty, administration and staff displayed as models to be emulated (Blackburn & Smith, 2010).

Further evidence of the heteronormativity of schools was revealed by Bower and Klecka (2009), who conducted a study (from a queer theory perspective) in which they explored the social norms possessed by teachers in the context of sexuality. Two of their key findings were that teachers generally "... operate within heteronormative frameworks" and the most dominant teacher norm was "... that educators do not contradict personal, moral, or religious beliefs of families" (p. 367). These results are not surprising since most schools operate in a heteronormative system within a heternormative society (Browne, Browne, & Lim, 2007).

Thus, educators have quite a task set before them: the dismantling of heteronormative frames via the utilization of anti-oppressive practices and pedagogies (Goldstein, Russell, & Daley, 2007; Grace & Wells, 2007; Kumashiro, 2002) so that oppression due to sexual orientation can no longer take place.

A Freirean Approach toward Reformational Dialogue

Clearly, our schools are in the midst of a crisis of dehumanization when anti-LGBT harassment and abuse occurs with such frequency and at such degree that the victims become "... so oppressed by dehumanizing social structures and conditions that they succumb to a sense of fatalism" (McInerney, 2009, p. 26). Paulo Freire's passion for social justice and his philosophies regarding oppression are sources of hope for many who witness or experience dehumanization. And although Freire was addressing oppression in a mostly socioeconomic context in his book, *Pedagogy of the Oppressed* (1970), we can apply his liberatory strategies in the context of the tragedy that is anti-LGBT harassment, abuse, and assault in our nation's schools.

Freire (1970) posited that dehumanization "... is the result of an unjust order that engenders violence in the oppressors, which in turn dehumanizes the oppressed" (p. 26). He further stated:

> Being less human leads the oppressed to struggle against those who made them so. In order for this struggle to have meaning, the oppressed must not, in seeking to regain their humanity (which is a way to create it), become in turn oppressors of the oppressors, but rather restorers of the humanity of both.
>
> This, then, is the great humanistic and historical task of the oppressed: to liberate themselves and their oppressors as well. The oppressors, who oppress, exploit, and rape, by virtue of their power, cannot find in this power the strength to liberate either the oppressed or themselves. Only power that springs from the weakness of the oppressed will be sufficiently strong to free both. (p. 26)

It is important to note that not all LGBT youth feel oppressed; in fact, Morris (2005) posits that much LGBT (now collectively known as queer) thinking and activism has made a shift to "parody, acting out, acting up, rude, and ludic performance" (p. 10). But for those LGBT youth who do feel oppressed, liberation could come from a Freirean perspective.

Freire (1970) indicated that the first steps toward liberation must be made by the oppressed and their authentic allies because it is only the oppressed who truly understand what it is like to exist in an oppressive society, and it is only the oppressed who understand the absolute necessity for liberation. Freire cautioned, however, against attempts to weaken the oppressors' power. In such instances what results is false generosity or false charity, which serves to "... constrain the fearful and subdue, the 'rejects of life,' to extend their trembling hands" (p. 27). Oppressors will go to great measures to maintain injustice, even perpetuating it themselves so that they can continue as powerful "generosity" givers.

It is only when the oppressors relinquish their charity work and instead work tirelessly together with the oppressed in a true partnership toward a mission to liberate that authentic transformation takes place. Freire (1970) also warned that this working partnership between oppressed and oppressor is only successful when initiated by the oppressed and their allies, and as the oppressed fight "... for the restoration of their humanity they will be attempting the restoration of true generosity" (p. 27). So not only do the oppressed initiate the conversation, they assume "... total responsibility for the struggle" (p. 50).

Unfortunately, at least in the beginning stages of the struggle, the oppressed, in their quest for liberation, themselves often become oppressors or "sub-oppressors." According to Freire (1970), this movement from oppressed to oppressor occurs because the oppressed have operated under the guidelines of the oppressors for so long that they have often internalized the guidelines, causing the oppressed to become fearful of their own liberation. To fully liberate themselves the oppressed must reject the urge to adopt the guidelines of the oppressor, and instead they must work to "... replace them with autonomy and responsibility" (p. 27). This is accomplished, according to Friere, by utilizing the pedagogy of the oppressed, beginning with its first stage, which requires the oppressed "... unveil the world of oppression and through the praxis commit themselves to its transformation" (p. 36).

A Dialogical Meeting

Therefore, applying the first stage of Freire's (1970) pedagogy to the problem of oppression of LGBT youth must involve a request by the oppressed (LGBT students)—because for success, the oppressed must initiate the need for action—for an assembly of LGBT youth, their peers, and teachers for a dialogue about the issue. There is some preparatory foundational cognition required of the oppressed though before the dialogue can commence.

They must first recognize that, through their oppression, they "... have been destroyed precisely because their situation has reduced them to things;" they cannot effectively "... enter into the struggle" without this acknowledgement (p. 50). Once the oppressed acknowledge their existence as objects rather than subjects and realize that they have been dehumanized, they must then commit to taking complete responsibility for the forthcoming struggle and enter into the struggle as humans for their own humanization (Freire, 1970).

Once a dialogical meeting is called, and stakeholders are present, the setting should ideally be arranged in such a way that oppressed and oppressors face one another at the same physical level (preferably in a circular fashion) so that the oppressed become subjects rather than objects in the environment and to facilitate looking inward together toward a shared concentration.

Identifying and Describing the Problem

Next, the oppressed must open a dialogue by identifying and describing the problem for reflection. Ideally, a few LGBT student leaders (Friere's revolutionaries) would begin the discussion by naming the problem (revealing it) and by personalizing it for the oppressors and sharing their individual experiences of harassment, discrimination, and abuse, and including how those experiences have influenced their self-esteem, educational progress, feelings of safety at school, health and well-being, world-views, consciousness, and ethics.

Freire (1970) stated:

> It is only when the oppressed find the oppressor out and become involved in the organized struggle for their liberation that they begin to believe in themselves. This discovery cannot be purely intellectual but must involve action; nor can it be limited to mere activism, but must include serious reflection; only then will it be a praxis. (p. 47)

Oppressed individuals must include authentic reflection as they describe their experiences (objects), for as Freire states, "... to speak a true word is to transform the world" (p. 87) by naming the reality (reflection) and altering it (action). It is also critical that the language of the oppressed incorporate humility, faith in humanization, equality, hope, love for the world, and critical thinking. This humanization of the dialogue allows for a horizontal (equitable) relationship between oppressed and oppressors—without humanization the dialogue becomes hierarchical (vertical and oppressive). The oppressed should also encourage oppressors to examine and share their own consciousness, "... their behavior, their view of the world, and their ethics" (p. 37), and encourage questions, commentary and critical object engagement (Freire, 1970). This Freirean methodology provides an opportunity for both oppressors and the oppressed to become empowered to experience transformative knowledge.

Using a Mediator

An interesting addition to consider for Freire's methodology toward critical consciousness is the utilization of a mediator (one who acts at the middle level of an intervention), as is often used in victim offender mediation programs. Schehr (2000) posited that such mediators (completely objective non-stakeholders) should not remain neutral parties, but rather should enter into the dialogue by creating spaces for the deconstruction and reconstruction of harm in the context of schools as cultural institutions while empowering the oppressed within the dialogue.

Friere (1985), referred to this as conscientization, a process whereby the oppressed "... achieve a deepening awareness both of the sociocultural reality that shapes their lives and of their capacity to transform that reality" (p. 93). Thus, mediators in this context would be known as transformative mediators, whose goal would be to empower both parties. Bush and Folger (1994) identify two means by which transformative mediators might empower both oppressed and oppressors: (1) listening during the dialogue for opportunities for those involved to make decisions that will empower them in the context of the conflict, and (2) encouraging and supporting stakeholders in the careful deliberation of any options available for resolution.

According to Freire (1970), "In the second stage, in which the reality of the oppression has already been transformed, this pedagogy ceases to belong to the oppressed and becomes a pedagogy of all people in the process of permanent liberation" (p. 36). At this point, the oppressed and oppressors enter into a co-intentional relationship where both are subjects working together to "... re-create knowledge" and in the process "... discover themselves as its permanent re-creators" (p. 51).

How Schools are Responding

Many school systems have finally recognized that the bullying of LGBT students is unacceptable and have begun to implement various programs and strategies to counteract such behavior. Unfortunately, many of these strategies are isolationistic, oppositional to what we know about the hidden curriculum, non-transformational, and counteract Freire's work.

For example, in response to the bullying of LGBT students, some districts have opted to open schools that primarily serve LGBT students who have been identified as high risk for dropping out of the educational system. One such initiative is the Harvey Milk School, supported by the Hetrick-Martin Institute, a gay-rights youth advocacy organization, that opened in 1985 in New York City. The school's mission is to "... establish and promote a community of successful, independent learners by creating a safe educational environment for all young people" (as cited in Bethard, R., 2002, p. 419). In addition, in Milwaukee in 2004, a gay-friendly school called Alliance opened its doors.

The removal of LGBT youth from traditional school settings does help ensure their safety, but the action is itself heteronormative, and classifies these individuals as so radically different from their heterosexual peers, that they must be schooled in a completely different setting. It does not address the behavior of the harassers; it removes the "cultural space for possibility" (Margolis, Soldatenko, Acker, & Gair, 2001, p. 15) in which the possibility for transformational dialogue could occur. Sadly, the outcomes of these efforts are that the harassers' homophobia is reinforced.

Somewhat more hopeful, but still not in line with Freire's approach, is Project 10, a counseling and education program that addresses the needs of LGBT youth, that was tested in 1985 at Fairfax High School in Los Angeles in response to a gay student's decision to quit school due to repeated harassment. Project 10 is an initiative that provides school staff training on LGBT youth issues, funds to purchase library materials related to LGBT concerns, assistance with nondiscrimination compliance, and various other services, none of which appear to encourage dialogue between LGBT youth and their heterosexual peers and teachers that might spur transformational change.

In addition, the literature is rife with many other recommendations to address LGBT mistreatment in the school setting (Jeltova & Fish, 2005; McFarland, 2001; Munoz-Plaza, Quinn, & Ronds, 2002; Winter, 2008). Graybill et. al. (2009) recommend:

> First, educators should include LGBT issues in the curriculum to increase the visibility and accomplishments of the population. Second, advocates should provide staff development related to LGBT issues. Third, advocates should support the organization of a gay-straight alliance (GSA), or an after school student club, to provide a safe space for LGBT students and their heterosexual allies. Fourth, sexual orientation should be included in existing antidiscrimination policies. Fifth, the visibility of LGBT populations should be increase by displaying supportive posters and resource fliers around school, in addition to including LGBT-related media in school libraries. (p. 571)

Numerous other recommendations have been made, including (a) schools establishing LGBT Parent Affinity Groups, (b) planning and delivering events that serve to deconstruct heteronormativity (such as an event that celebrates all family types), (c) informing new hires of the expectation to support LGBT students and their families (Winter, 2008), (d) offering "safe spaces" where LGBT students can go for counseling and encouragement (Mayberry, 2006), (e) naming a particular school administrator to handle all anti-LGBT complaints,

(f) establishing a student sexual orientation confidentiality policy of nondisclosure for all school workers, (g) providing specialized training related to issues specific to LGBT students for guidance and counseling staff, (h) developing recommended reading lists that include texts on gay issues, (i) having information available for LGBT students and their families regarding local resources and organizations that support or aid LGBT youth, (j) maintaining gender neutral dress codes, and (k) evaluating curricular materials for discrimination and stereotyping (Human Rights Watch, 2001). While all of these recommendations are steps in the right direction, and many of the recommended strategies will decrease LGBT bullying, none serve to liberate the oppressed.

Summary

LGBT youth represent a population in schools at risk to bullying in and by the schools. Evidence does suggest that the practice is widespread and emanates from both peers and professional staff. We have examined some of the causes of maintenance structures for this current climate and forcefully argued for immediate change in policies and activities to protect students.

But going a step further, we conclude that true liberation and acceptance cannot be attained by these policies alone. Indeed, from a Freirean perspective, many common and apparently well intentioned practices actually support and extend the misbehaviors directed toward LGBT. But this is unnoticed as separation reduces surface conflict.

Perhaps we have seen this phenomenon before in schools and failed to take heed from the outcomes. In many ways the initial civil rights struggles associated with school integration followed similar paths in bullying and the reduction of full humanity. Only when integration in schools began to take hold was an actual dialogue across racial perspectives achieved.

In addition, the struggles of LGBT are not dissimilar from the struggle to educate special needs students with others. The current push for inclusion masks the decades of self contained classes and outright denial of services in public schools. There is no doubt special needs students suffered bullying and only with the advent of litigation and legislation has this been reduced as proximity with normal (general education) peers became the norm.

Progress in both of these instances followed closely the requirements described by Freire (1970). We find this abbreviated history of previous instances of bullying and harassment distressing, and yet, potentially comforting. It is certainly a distressing event because it seems difference promotes a negative response, including bullying and abuse, and seemingly we have difficulty learning from previous events. But both situations, the integration of students by race and full inclusion for special needs services, have been initiated and continue to evolve.

In many places integration, unquestioned acceptance, full acknowledgement of basic rights and privileges are the norm and, as we look forward, will certainly become the norm. Can it be otherwise for LGBT? We think not, and that is, we believe, a comforting precedent.

References

Bethard, R. (2002). New York's Harvey Milk School: A viable alternative. *Journal of Law and Education, 33*(3), 417–423.

Blackburn, M. V., & Smith, J. M. (2010). Moving beyond the inclusion of LGBT-themed literature in English language arts classrooms: Interrogating heteronormativity and exploring intersectionality. *Journal of Adolescent and Adult Literacy, 53*(8), 625–634. doi:10.1598/JAAL.53.8.1

Bower, L., & Klecka, C. (2009). (Re)considering normal: queering social norms for parents and teachers. *Teaching Education, 20*(4), 357–373. Doi:10.1080/10476210902862605

Browne, G., Browne, K., & Lim, J. (2007). Introduction or Why have a book on geographies of sexualities? In K. Browen, J. Lim, & G. Brown (Eds.), *Geographies of sexualities: Theory, practices and politics* (pp. 1–20). Aldershot, UK: Ashgate.

Bush, R. B., & Folger, J. P. (1994). *The promise of mediation: Responding to conflict through empowerment and recognition.* San Francisco: Jossey-Bass.

Buston, K., & Hart, G. (2001). Heterosexuals' use of "fag" and "queer" to deride one another: A contributor to heterosexism and stigma. *Journal of Homosexuality, 40*(2), 1–11.

California Safe Schools Coalition. (2004). *Consequences of harassment based on actual or perceived sexual orientation and gender non-conformity and steps for making schools safer.* Davis, CA: University of California.

Carter, K. (1997). Gay slurs abound. *The Des Moines Register,* March 7, 1997, p. 1.

Chambers, D., van Loon, J., & Tincknell, E. (2004). Teachers' views of teenage sexual morality. *British Journal of Sociology of Education, 25*(5), 563–76. doi:10.1080/0142569042000252053

Cody. (n.d). Re: The effects of prejudice in schools [online forum comment]. Retrieved from http://www.avert.org/gay-school.htm

Dani. (n.d.). Re: The effects of prejudice in schools [online forum comment]. Retrieved from http://www.avert.org/gay-school.htm

Dylan, B. (1964). My back pages. On *Another side of Bob Dylan* (record). New York: Columbia Records.

Flores vs. Morgan Hill United School District, 324 F.3d 1130 (9th Cir. 2003)

Freire, P. (1970). *Pedagogy of the oppressed.* New York: Continuum Publishing.

Friere, P. (1985). *The politics of education: Culture, power, and liberation.* South Hadley, MA: Bergin & Garvey.

Foucault, M. (1978). *The history of sexuality* (Vol. 1). (R. Hurley, Trans.). New York: Random House.

Gary. (n.d.). Re: The effects of prejudice in schools [online forum comment]. Retrieved from http://www.avert.org/gay-school.htm

Gay, Lesbian, and Straight Education Network (GLSEN). (1999). *National school climate survey*. New York: Author.

Gay, Lesbian, and Straight Education Network (GLSEN). (2005). *National school climate survey*. New York: Author.

Gay, Lesbian, and Straight Education Network (GLSEN) and Harris Interactive. (2005). *From teasing to torment: School climate in America, a survey of students and teachers*. New York: GLSEN.

Goldstein, T., Russell, V., & Daley, A. (2007). Safe, positive and queering moments in teaching education and schooling: A conceptual framework. *Teaching Education, 18*, 183–199. Doi:10.1080/10476210701533035

Grace, A., & Wells, K. (2007). Using Freirean pedagogy of Just Ire to inform critical social learning in arts-informed community education for sexual minorities. *Adult Education Quarterly, 57*, 95–114. Doi:10.1177/0741713606294539

Graybill, E. C., Varjas, K., Meyers, J., & Watson, L. (2009). Content-specific strategies to advocate for lesbian, gay, bisexual, and transgender youth: An exploratory study. *School Psychology Review, 38*(4), 570–584.

Human Rights Watch. (2001). *Hatred in the hallways: Violence and discrimination against lesbian, gay, bisexual, and transgender students in U.S. schools*. New York: Author.

Jeltova, I., & Fish, M. C. (2005). Creating school environments responsive to gay, lesbian, bisexual, and transgender families: Traditional and systemic approaches for consultation. *Journal of Educational and Psychological Consultation, 16*, 17–33. Doi:10.1207/s1532768xjepc161&2_2

Jordan, K. M., Vaughan, J. S., & Woodworth, K. J. (1997). I will survive: Lesbian, gay and bisexual youths' experience of high school. *Journal of Gay and Lesbian Social Services, 7*(4), 17–33.

Kosciw, J. G. & Cullen, M. (2001). *The GLSEN 2001 National School Climate Survey: The school-related experiences of our nation's lesbian, gay, bisexual, and transgender youth*. New York: The Office for Public Policy of the Gay, Lesbian, and Straight Education Network.

Kosciw, J. G., & Diaz, E. M. (2006). *The 2005 National School Climate Survey: The experiences of lesbian, gay, bisexual, and transgender youth in our nation's schools*. New York: Gay, Lesbian and Straight Education Network. Retrieved November 18, 2010 from http://www.glsen.org

Kumashiro, K. (2002). *Troubling education: Queer activism and anti-oppressive pedagogy*. New York: Rutledge Falmer.

Margolis, E., Soldatenko, M., Acker, S., & Gair, M. (2001). Hiding and outing the curriculum. In E. Margolis (Ed.), *The hidden curriculum in higher education* (pp. 1–19). New York: Routledge.

Mayberry, M. (2006). School reform efforts for lesbian, gay, bisexual, and transgendered students. *The Clearing House, 79*(6), 262–264. Doi:10.3200/TCHS.79.6.262-264

McFarland, W. P. (2001). The legal duty to protect gay and lesbian students from violence in school. *Professional School Counseling, 4,* 171–178.

McInerney, P. (2009). Toward a critical pedagogy of engagement for alienated youth: Insights from Freire and school-based research. *Critical Studies in Education, 50*(1), 23–35. doi:10.1080/17508480802526637

Meyer, E. J. (2008). Gendered harassment in secondary schools: Understanding teachers' (non) interventions. *Gender and Education, 20*(6), pp. 555–570. doi:10.1080/09540250802213115

Morris, M. (2005). Queer life and school culture: Troubling genders. *Multicultural Education, 12*(3), pp. 8–13.

Munoz-Plaza, C., Quinn, S. C., & Rounds, K. A. (2002). Lesbian, gay, bisexual and transgender students: Perceived social support in the high school environment. *The High School Journal,* (Apr/May). doi:10.1353/hsj.2002.0011

Nansel, T. R., Overpeck, M., Pilla, R. S., Ruan, W. J., Simons-Morton, B., & Scheidt, P. (2001). Bullying behaviors among U.S. youth: Prevalence and association with psychological adjustment. *Journal of American Medical Association, 285*(16), 2094–2100. doi:10.1001/jama.285.16.2094

Pellegrini, A. d., Bartini, M., & Brooks, F. (2001). School bullies, victims, and aggressive victims: Factors relating to group affiliation and victimization in early adolescence. *Journal of Educational Psychology, 91,* 216–224.

Peters, A. J. (2003). Isolation or inclusion: Creating safe spaces for lesbian and gay youth. *Families in Society: The Journal of Contemporary Human Services, 84,* 85–110.

Renold, E. (2000). "Coming out": Gender (hetero)sexuality and the primary school. *Gender and Education, 12*(3), 309–326. doi:10.1080/713668299

Rich, A. (1980). Compulsory heterosexuality and lesbian existence. *Signs: Journal of Women in Culture and Society, 5*(4), 631–660. doi:10.1086/493756

Robinson, K. H., & Ferfolja, T. (2008). Playing it up, playing it safe: Queering teacher education. *Teaching and Teacher Education, 24,* 846–858. Doi:10.1016/j.tate.2007.11.004

Schehr, R.C. (2000). From restoration to transformation: Victim-offender mediation as transformative justice. *Conflict Resolution Quarterly, 18*(20, 151–169. Doi:10.1002/crq.3890180205

Shor, I., & Freire, P. (1987). *A pedagogy for liberation: Dialogues on transforming education.* Westport, CT: Bergin & Garvey.

Stockdale, M. S., Hangaduambo, S., Duys, D., Larson, K., & Sarvela, P.D. (2002). Rural elementary students', parents', and teachers' perceptions of bullying. *American Journal of Health Behavior, 26,* 266–277.

U.S. Department of Education and U.S. Department of Justice. (2006). *Indicators of school crime and safety.* Washington, DC: Authors.

Wilson, I., Griffin, C., & Wren, B. (2005). The interaction between young people with atypical gender identity organization and their peers. *Journal of Health Psychology, 10*(3), 307–15. Doi:10.1177/1359105305051417

Winter, E. (2008). The new constituency: Welcoming LGBT-headed families into our schools. *Independent Schools, 68*(1), 95–99.

CPSIA information can be obtained
at www.ICGtesting.com
Printed in the USA
LVHW101914090921
697471LV00003B/9